A Pilot's Story

Selections from the diary of a fighter pilot's 93 missions in the European Theater in World War II

By
Irwin D. Lebow

Richard,
Hope you enjoy my stories

[signature]
5/15/22

First printing

Printed in the United States of America

Acknowledgement

Thanks to my son Barry whose countless hours of technical assistance made this book possible. Also to my brother Morty whose advice and his submission of my diary to the Library of Congress gave official recognition to this book. To Ron, Deborah, Nancy and Pat for their encouragement to get this done and to my wife of 76 years, Judy, my best friend, for her love and constant support

May 2, 1961

On this 20th anniversary of the first flight of the
P-47 Thunderbolt fighter aircraft, it's designer
and producer, the Republic Aviation Corporation,
of Farmingdale, New York is honored to present
this commemorative scroll to

Irwin Lebow

Who, in the service of his country did, during
World War II, pilot a P-47 Thunderbolt
with courage and distinction

Mundy A. Peale
President
Republic Aviation Corporation

Entered combat March 1943
Served in all active theatres except Alaska
Flew 549,575 sorties; 1,350,810 combat hours
Destroyed 9,067 enemy aircraft

Destroyed or damaged:
86,000 railroad cars; 9,306 locomotives;
9,000 armored vehicles and tanks;
68,000 motor transports

In a ceremony at Republic Aviation factory on Long Island, N. Y. on the 20th anniversary of the P47 Thunderbolt's first flight, this certificate was presented to Irwin Lebow.

Introduction

When the United States was attacked by Japan I had a job as a tool and die makers apprentice in a defense plant. Not willing to wait to be drafted, I enlisted in the Army Air Corps to fulfill my dream of becoming a pilot. Leaving Judy my bride, I reported to Maxwell Field in Montgomery Alabama as an Aviation Cadet. Then followed a series of bases as I climbed the ladder acquiring new skills at each one.

First at Americus Georgia where I was introduced to flight training. Then Macon Georgia where I learned to fly an Advanced Trainer 6 closed cockpit plane. Then Moultrie Georgia where I finally completed my basic fight training and received my wings as a pilot. Then to Richmond Army Air base and Seymour Johnson Field in South Carolina for advanced training. Finally to Eglin Army Air Base in Florida for gunnery training flying a P47 Thunderbolt. It was there that my career as a pilot almost came to a disastrous end.

Flying over the Gulf of Mexico we would get our gunnery training while shooting at an airborne target. On one pass at the target my bullets hit the cable that connected it to the tow plane. The now disengaged target flew back slamming into the wing of my plane making it difficult to fly. Desperately calling the base, they advised me to bail out over the Everglades where they would pick me up in a day or two. Not willing to chance that, I informed the controller that I would try to make it back to the field. I was able to come in successfully and was escorted down the runway as I landed by fire trucks and ambulances.

It was after that incident that I had a week leave to go home and say my goodbyes to my wife, family and friends and then embarked on the USS General Megs troopship for Naples Italy. After landing I was sent to the island of Corsica to join the 27th Fighter Group, a group that had been sent to Pearl Harbor five days before the December 7th attack by the Japanese, where they had been wiped out. Reactivated in Savannah Ga. and then sent to support our troops in North Africa and then Italy and Corsica, where I joined them. The 27th was the only fighter group to receive 5 Presidential Citations.

Flying from airfields in Corsica, Italy, France and finally Germany I flew my P47 Thunderbolt on 93 missions over Italy, France and Germany from July 1944 until the end of the war in Europe on May 8th 1945, coming under attack from ground fire and enemy aircraft countless times. During that time I was the pilot chosen to fly the half millionth sortie for the 12th Air Force in the European Theatre of Operations. The mission was supposed to be an easy one so that we could dive bomb an Italian machine gun emplacement on the coast and then return to have our pictures taken with General Cannon for the news cameras. In the attack on the gun emplacements the pilot in front of me was shot down.

This is a story written by a 22 year young man being exposed to life and death situations on a daily basis, but also living with the thrill and excitement of doing things that movies are made of. As a fighter pilot, flying in a machine capable of delivering destruction was a thrilling experience. There are memories of returning from successful missions and climbing out of the cockpit on a high because of the destruction of enemy targets.

The "high" of successfully blowing up trains, tanks, vehicles and strafing enemy ground troops was shared by all of us. Because of the way we depended on each other there was also a special "esprit de corps" that was unique to our service.

My view of the war was, of course, different from those who fought the war on the ground. When I returned from a mission I still had a comfortable existence with dinner in safe surroundings and a bed to sleep in. Different then my younger brother who was in the Infantry and was wounded fighting the Germans.

This is my story taken from the diary which is on file at the Library of Congress in their Veteran's History Project archives.

Chapter 1 – July 1944
Naples

Friday, July 21

Had breakfast which was to be our last meal aboard ship. After breakfast, I went below and packed all my stuff, showered and shaved and went up to the lounge. It's hot as blazes and I felt very disgruntled and weak because of not enough to eat. While they were serving the noon meal to the civilians and French, I went to the Mess Hall and gyped 6 cans of C rations but decided to save them for some time when I may need them more than now.

Went topside just in time to see the Isle of Capri as we sailed past. All the romantic songs about it are the bunk because it is the most unromantic looking spot in the world. It is a huge rock about 4 miles square that sticks up out of the water. We saw one tree on it, a little grass and a few houses. Soon after we passed Capri we entered the harbor at Naples. It was packed with every type of ship known. We sailed very slowly through all the parked vessels and finally stopped about 1/2 mile out from shore and just sat there. They made the announcement that supper would be served. It turned out that it was a steak dinner which was really good. It was a nice farewell supper aboard ship.

On the way into the harbor we saw a couple of smashed up U-Boats and other ships all near the shore. As we moved closer to land, we could see plenty of bombed out buildings and loads of people living on the beaches. They were dirty, ragged and hungry looking. It was the kind of sight that sends chills up your spine.

At 1730 the ship moved into a pier and started tying up. The pier had at one time been a very nice looking terminal, but it was just a blasted ruin. All the army had done was to clear the wreckage enough so the pier was usable. While we were tying up, loads of Italian civilians came on the pier and were begging. They were the saddest looking lot I ever did see but yet I couldn't help feeling sorry for them. We threw cigarettes and candy to them. It was a pathetic sight.

About 1930 we prepared to debark. Mt. Vesuvius towers above us in all its splendor while we staggered down the gangway loaded with packs and bags. We waited in the terminal till about 2100 and then we found this truck that wasn't being used. We commandeered it and its Italian driver. We didn't trust the driver to get us anywhere safely so I told the Sgt. that I would drive the truck. He told the Italian driver that I was an "officialle." and he shined his flashlight on my gold bar. I gave the driver some cigarettes and then I was his "pizon." The boys piled in back and we were off. At first I ground gears because it was all new to me, but pretty soon I got the hang of it. We were having a hell of a time.

Naples has a 2130 curfew so all the streets were dark and MPs were everywhere but we rode all over town before we started looking for our base. This town smells awful and it really is beaten up. After riding around for about an hour, we finally found someone who knew where we were supposed to be so we took off again.

All the time I was feeding the Italian next to me candy and cigarettes to keep him quiet. Every once in a while he would rattle off some Italian and I would nod my head as if I understood very well.

We, finally, after riding up and down mountains, pulled into our camp which is a Replacement Pool. I let the Italian have his truck back then and I gave him a pack of cigarettes and a candy bar. We drew blankets and cots and mosquito nets and then went to our tent. This camp is only two months old and it has about 6 inches of dust everywhere you turn. We broke out our K Rations in the tent and had a party - lemonade and all. Unpacked and finally hit the sack at 0200. The night was beautiful and there were twice as many stars as there normally are, and I sure do miss my Judy.

Saturday, July 22

Awoke at 0530 because I was freezing and there was a lot of noise. The boys who had gotten off the boat with us were moving into camp. They had to walk all the way here. It really was a break our getting that truck. Breakfast was darn good. There are Italian boys working as waiters in the Officer's Mess and they are really on the ball. Gave the boy a cigarette as a tip. Went to classification and got myself checked in and then went to Finance and changed my money to lira. Had a meeting at 0930 and was told about censorship and a few post regulations. The C.O. said we would only be here about 2 days till we would be assigned to a Fighter Group, which is just fine.

Dick and I got a lift in a jeep to Caserta. Wandered around town for a while. Everything is bombed and broken up. There are a lot of barber shops and souvenir shops open but everything else is closed. Practically everyone on the streets was in the U.S. Army. The population is poor and very dirty looking.

Sunday, July 23

Awoke at 0730 and washed from a canteen. You never realize how much American people just take for granted. At home you turn on a tap and you have water, you flip a switch and you have light and turn on a radiator for heat. Water here is scarce and often rationed. You can wash surprising well with a canteen of water poured into a helmet. We have candles here to get us some light at night.

After breakfast Dick and I went over to get passes (Moose and Dick are guys I came over with), and I left camp about 1030 and caught a lift down the road to a big airport just outside of Naples. They've got every plane that there is on that field. We wandered around looking at planes for about an hour. That new P 47 is really a sweet looking airplane. Then we took off for Pompeii to see all the ruins there. As we started into the ruins, we were mobbed by kids selling everything under the sun. Some were selling souvenirs and others were selling their sisters. Finally got to the ruins and got a guide for 200 lira and spent 3 hours walking all over the place. It's amazing the paintings have been preserved over thousands of years. They must have used wonderful paint.

They also must have been great drinkers because every corner had a wine shop in it. Must have walked 10 miles looking that place over. Got a lift back to Naples in an RAF truck. Got to camp at 2230 and was asleep when my head touched the pillow.

Monday, July 24

Nothing to do again today. Went to the Officer's Club and wrote to Judy and home. At about 2000 the boys and I caught a lift to Caserta. We looked at the Palace for awhile and then it started to get dark so we headed back to camp. Stopped at a roadside stand and bargained with the Italian and finally got a load of fruit for 50 lira.

Tuesday, July 25

We have been alerted that we might get our assignments today and we are all hoping to move although I doubt it. Was getting ready to go swimming when Stevens, one of the guys we came over with, rushed in with word that we were leaving at 1500. We immediately started packing and cleaning up. We didn't leave until 1600. Dick is being shipped to another squadron and I sure hate to lose that guy. We had gone through most of our training together. He sure is a good egg.

We found that they are flying us over to Corsica by C47. We went to the airport across the road at 1700 and loaded our baggage and ourselves aboard and we were ready to go. The pilot let us take turns flying the tub.

Corsica

The trip from Caserta to Corsica took only 2 hours where it would have taken 1 1/2 days by truck and boat. We landed and were met by Col. Mack the C.O. of the 27th Fighter Group, who seems like a good egg. We loaded our luggage from the plane to a truck and drove to our group area. Had an orientation lecture that took most of the morning.

Lt. Brown, the officer in charge, told us all about what we are going to be doing and how we are going to do it. He also gave us a short history of this Fighter Group, and for a change, I think I am getting into a good outfit. From all the talk around here there seems to be another invasion force ready to move, probably to the coast of France around Marseilles. They've gotten lots of wing tanks so that means long trips. I hear that some of the flights have been going on fighter swings into France. I must admit that the thought of flying in combat scares me but I'm still anxious to get started. These boys here are doing a swell job of dive bombing and strafing German supply lines.

After chow we had a meeting with the Col. He walked around the Group and introduced himself. He just wants us to stay on the ball, but if we screw up, we're going to get hell. We were assigned to Squadrons. Neilson, Reasman, Reece (the guys I came over with) and I are in the 524th Fighter Bomber Squadron. Most missions are dive bombing and strafing with very few escort missions.

The squadron here was specially glad to have us here, because they knew we were already well trained in the P47. We'll get a couple of rides before we go on missions. We're supposed to fly this afternoon after an escape lecture. We were told what, how and when to do things if we were ever forced down behind enemy lines. Most of the men who are forced down eventually work their way back, which is very encouraging.

We then went to our squadron ready tent where we were fitted for our parachutes and our, May West's (special inflatable vests you wear when flying over water) which are English made and pretty neat. Then got my oxygen mask fitted with a mike and got my helmet fixed up. Got some time in a P47, and before we knew it, it was supper time. After supper, we borrowed a Jeep and picked up more packing cases to use as floors and closets in our tent. We're going to make that place real cozy.

Thursday, July 27th

Went to the Pilots Ready Tent and got our equipment ready because we were going to fly this morning. I must admit that I was nervous as hell and a little scared but more because I'll do something wrong than because I might get hurt. We took off at 1030 and I flew over the Elba and buzzed hell out of it. It's mountainous as hell and it was really fun flying around it. Got the feel of the plane again and really started to enjoy it. The name of the plane was "Miss Judy" and it really is a great airplane. My honey is lucky for me. Coming in to land the tower was yelling so that I couldn't understand a word, but as I was ready to set the plane down they shot a red flare in front of me and in front of a B25 coming in the opposite direction.

We both shoved our throttle full forward and just missed each other. I was sweating bullets and my heart was pounding hard enough for everyone on the ground to hear it. Went around and came in and landed long and had to use plenty of brake to stop at the end of the runway. That ride was piss poor but I'm beginning to feel at home in the cockpit again.

After lunch we went up again and I really enjoyed myself and felt very much at home in the cockpit. I buzzed every nearby island and came across the water to Corsica on the deck. Made a nice landing and when I taxied in the crew chief told me that I may get that airplane for myself. I was really tickled when I heard that because it is a brand new plane.

I had supper and then Reece and I decided to get some more packing cases to use in fixing our tent up. We started one truck and barely got it moving into the road when the motor quit. No gas. Reece started another truck to use in pushing our empty one off the road and he pushed it into a ditch, accidently of course, so there we were with two disabled trucks blocking the road. A G.I. came along in a truck and helped us straighten things out.

Friday, July 28th

Got some packing cases to use for our tent. Spent the morning making a table and getting ready to lay the floor. Reece and I went to Bastia this afternoon. This whole island is terribly beaten up and Bastia is in ruins. Drove around the town for awhile and after we got tired, drove back to camp. French is the only language spoken on this island so I'm hoping to improve mine. Then we started to lay the floor in our tent.

The Aviation Engineers are going to lay a steel mat so that we will have a good runway. The name of this place is Sersage Field, home of the 27th Flight Group.

Saturday, July 29

Woke at 7:45. Today is nice and cool for a change. Just sat around till lunchtime relaxing. After lunch, we took a truck and drove around picking up more empty crates to use for the tent. Spent most of the afternoon finishing the floor and then took a short nap before supper. The tent really looks good with its nice wooden floor and everyone who passes by stops to admire it.

Had supper and then all the new pilots had a meeting with the colonel. He really gave us hell because a few of the new boys screwed up on transition flights One got lost and landed near Rome and another one was caught doing spins with a P47 which is just sticking your neck out.

After the meeting, we went to the mess hall and got a snack to eat and then went to our outdoor movie. "Chip Off the Old Block" which was very entertaining. Hit the sack at about midnight. I'm so tired at the end of each day that I fall asleep as soon as I get into bed.

The field was closed today and will be closed for the next few days while the steel landing mat is put down. Reasman was taken to the hospital today for what they think is appendicitis.

Sunday, July 30

After breakfast went to the Ready Tent and had a discussion on formations and tactics. Everything is figured out. All we have to do is to act fast in an emergency.

After lunch we went down to the flight line and had our pictures taken with our airplane. They are supposed to be sent to our home town newspapers so that everyone can see what a fine job we're doing.

Monday, July 31

Spent the morning getting lectures on escape and our tactics. Went down to the flight line at 1330 and we were briefed on formation flying. Then we all went out to our airplanes. Started up and taxied out and took off. We lined up pretty nicely and then started flying out toward Italy. We held a pretty fair line abreast formation and we practiced breaks which are pretty exciting and fast as hell. You really have to be on your toes. A break is called whenever an enemy plane is sighted. Its purpose is to swing the formation so that all guns are pointed at the enemy. When the break is called every man swings into the right place immediately. It really is a nice maneuver and after a few tries we were doing it pretty well.

Our leader then put us in an echelon right, which is the formation where we line up in one line to dive on the target and he peeled off to practice dive bombing. When we start the dive we have to turn the plane over so that we can see the target we will be diving on. We went off right after him and each man held good position.

I was "tail end Charlie" on the right and when I peeled off and covered the other 3 ships up ahead of me on the dive it was really a beauty. We went tearing down at about 400 mph and came out right on the deck where we reformed and buzzed for awhile. Came in and peeled off and landed. For a change made a sweet landing. I hardly felt the wheels touch. That was really a swell flight and we all enjoyed it.

We found a dog in our tent when we came back. He was a cute little fellow so we let him sleep on Reasman's sack.

Chapter 2 - August 1944

Tuesday, August 1

Went to breakfast and then to the Flight Line. Took off on another practice formation flight. Went to the Italian mainland and buzzed for about 15 minutes. That felt really good. We were never higher than 20 feet and we were just over the brush. We scared hell out of a farmer and his cows. They are all running like mad as we came over. He must have thought the end had come. Came back and had lunch and relaxed by reading and writing.

Our squadron doesn't have anything scheduled for the rest of the afternoon so everyone is taking it easy. About 1610 we found out that one of the Warrant Officers was driving to Bastia so Neilson and I went with him. He drove like hell and made good time into town. The PX had beer so we were able to get 18 bottles by using 3 ration cards. We loaded all the stuff into the jeep and hid it because we were going to leave the jeep outside.

After supper Neilson and I went to the Red Cross Officers Club and got haircuts. I got mine nice and short for a change. There isn't anyone here to complain about it being too short. We went to the harbor and watched the patrol boats come in for the night. They are ugly looking tubs.

Finally headed back to camp. On the way we passed an auto accident. Four G.I'.s had driven a truck off a 50 foot cliff and naturally killed themselves. We got back to camp at 2230 to find Reece very P.O.'d. He had taken his gun apart to clean it and couldn't get it together again.

We found out that two generals were visiting Corsica today which means something is up. This island has 16 airfields and it seems that it is a keg of dynamite. They expect trouble here and they also expect another invasion pretty soon. Everyone is trying to figure out where it will be. I'm sure it's going to be Southern France because our squadron has been doing a lot of bombing there lately. Everyone can feel the tension and we all know something big is coming soon.

Wednesday, August 2

After lunch, Neilson and Reece went on their first mission. They were out to bomb a bridge near Turin, Italy.   I envy them because I'm still sweating my first mission and I can't help being a little scared. I just want to get it over with. The boys come back from every mission as if it was a lot of fun and they never seem to lose anyone.

We had a questionnaire to fill out on the P47 and then a few of us went down the line to fly a practice bombing mission. Before we took off, we had a bull session with one of the squadron leaders and he said we have one week to get some practice in night flying, learn to take care of our own airplane and guns. That means something big is popping pretty soon. We took off on our mission and practice bombed the target. On our way home we had a pretty good rat race over the mountain and then we put on a show over the field. We barrel rolled all over the sky and we all landed feeling good.

There was a meeting of all pilots going on when we came in so we quietly took our places. It seems that someone on the morning mission screwed up and no one wants to take the blame.

They all got hell for it and it seems that the squadron leaders are going to tighten down on all pilots. It doesn't affect us new sports yet.

Found out that I am on the first mission tomorrow morning. I'm a little nervous about it. More because I hope I do everything right than because I'm afraid of getting hurt. Went back and ate supper and then Reece and I had target practice with our 45s. We knocked up a tin can pretty well.

Thursday, August 3

Had breakfast and got to the Flight Line at 0745 where we were briefed for the mission. We are carrying 2 five hundred pound bombs and our target is a bridge in France near Nice. The bridge is at the end of a narrow valley which is surrounded by tall mountains which means we have to let our bombs go from pretty high up.

Turned in all my papers and my wallet and was given an escape kit and went out to our airplanes. We took off at 0845 and I flew in White Flight as the leader's wingman. We got off O.K. but something was wrong with our leader's plane and he had to go back. So the element leader took over and one of us flew on each of his wings. I was sweating a blue streak trying to stay in formation, but thank god, I was too busy to be nervous.

We got to the target in 45 minutes and circled it twice. There was no flak at all. We peeled off and I saw bombs explode on the bridge while I was in my dive. I let my bombs go at about 7,000 feet and started pulling out. I don't think I hit anything.

We reformed and took evasive action and then headed straight for home. The Red Cross gals were there with coffee and donuts for us. We were interrogated and came back to our tents. The mission was an easy one but even so, I'm glad I'm past mission #1 successfully. After lunch we had to get back to the line to take care of our own airplanes.

Came back from the line at 1630 and went to see Captain Brucker, the Group Dentist, about why my gums have been bleeding so much lately. I have an impacted wisdom tooth he said that will have to come out pretty soon. I stayed there until suppertime talking to him. He's a very nice guy who knows my section of NY pretty well.

Friday, August 4

Went to see the dentist again. He gave me some dope to deaden the pain in my tooth and then had me grounded for the rest of the day. He was trying to get a ride to Rome today and asked me to drive him up to the next scheduled flight and bring the jeep back. I went along and enjoyed the ride.

While I was waiting for him, I walked down to the beach. It reminded me so much of Rockaway that I felt very homesick. The Captain couldn't find the person he was looking for so we headed back. We detoured so that I could stop at the hospital to see Reasman who is doing fine and should be back and start flying soon.

Saturday, August 5

Nothing much doing this morning so I got ambitious and built a rack to hang my mosquito net over. Finished at about 1530 when we suddenly heard a crash out at the end of the runway.

The pilot was a new sport. He stalled out at about 100 feet in the air and the plane rolled over onto its back and then crashed and caught fire. We went over to the wreck and it was scattered over 1/2 mile on the ground. The pilot and the seat he was in was thrown about 100 feet from the plane and half his head was off. It was a horrible sight.

Sunday, August 6

Went to the group Operations Tent to see how the war is going. The Russians are only 325 miles from Berlin. I hope the Russians get there first and give the Nazis a good dose of their own medicine so that we'll have no fear of war from them for the next 50 years.

Was notified of a mission this noon. At 1100 we went down to the flight line and got our briefing. Our target is a road through the mountains north of Nice. We are to bomb the road out. The weather isn't too good but we're going anyway. We took off at 1245 carrying two 500 pounders and a belly tank. We went through some low clouds when we crossed over the mountains on Corsica, and it was a pretty horrible feeling when you are flying 50 feet from another plane and he suddenly disappears.

We came out on top in pretty good formation. When we got over the continent our target was obscured by clouds. We couldn't take a chance on going down because of the mountains. As we neared the coast, we found a hole in the clouds so we went down and bombed a town and then flew back to Sarregio Field landing at 1445 and was interrogated. Came back to the tent and took a nap before supper. After supper Reece and I took target practice. I hit 5 beer bottles in six shots which is better than I've ever done.

Today is the 27th anniversary of the Army Air Force and orders came down from the high command that all groups had to fly a maximum number of missions regardless of the weather. So that's what we did. Formation flying all day. It was an awful waste of gas, bullets and bombs, because 90% of the missions couldn't reach their targets because of bad weather but it will probably look good in the newspapers back home.

Monday, August 7

Was awakened at 0700 because I was on the first mission. Went to the flight line at 0730 and was briefed. Our target was a railroad bridge in the Po Valley. We were carrying a belly tank and two 1000 pound bombs. Took off at 0845 and the plane is like an old horse with so much weight on it. We joined formation and flew toward Italy climbing all the way.

We sighted plenty of friendly aircraft but no Jerries at all. Found our target and peeled off for our bombing run. I was 11th man down on the target. By then it was all covered with smoke and dust so I let my bombs go toward the center of the cloud. There were several towns nearby but we got no flak at all so we circled the target before going home. Couldn't see too much due to the tremendous clouds of smoke and dust, but we sure did hit our bridge.

Flew home and when we got there had to circle for 1/2 hour because of so many planes landing ahead of us. Finally got down and was interrogated. After lunch I caught a truck to Bastia. Stopped at the Finance Office and got paid a tremendous $38.50 for the month of July. Our squadron has the next day and a half off so I don't have to get up till 0830 for breakfast.

Tuesday, August 8

After lunch went over to supply and drew a mattress roll. They are a new type of sleeping bag with a zipper all around.

The boys and I all rode up to the hospital to see Reasman. He's doing fine and he'll be back in about a week. Drove up to Cervionne, a small mountain town which is quite quaint and then back to camp and supper after which I read and reread my mail. Four letters from my honey and one from home. That mail is wonderful stuff. Had a snack at 2130 and then hit the sack eager to try out my new sleeping bag.

Wednesday, August 9

Was able to get some extra sacktime because the weather was not too good. Borrowed Doc's jeep and went and had a nice hot shower and then went to a pilots meeting at 1530. We were told that the way things stand we have to get at least 100 missions before we can go home. General Eaker may change that, but until he does that's how things stand. Found out that Nave didn't come back from his first mission. I really got a chill from that.

Thursday, August 10

After breakfast there was a meeting with our Operations Officer and he informed us that pilots would not have to spend time waiting at the flight line if they did not have a mission scheduled. It seems that there had been a rule that pilots should always be available on short notice. I'm on a mission this afternoon and what a mission that will be. It's a 24 ship mission and we are going after a radar station in France. I'll get all the details later. Unfortunately it was pouring when it came time for the mission so it was called off.

Friday, August 11

That big mission is coming up this afternoon. I'm kind of nervous about it but not as scared as I was yesterday. Three o'clock came and we all went down to the line for a pilots meeting. At 1600 our briefing started. Our target is a pinpoint target, a radar station near Marseilles. We had 20 planes to bomb and four planes for top cover in case the enemy came up. We carried 36 fragmentation bombs each and we got orders to strafe all the way down, because there were a lot of enemy gun positions around the station. Everyone was a little nervous because we expected trouble. We went out to the planes at 1630 and took off.

We had to circle the field twice to give everyone a chance to get into formation. We had to maintain a strict radio silence and flew at about 30 feet over the water so that the Jerry radar couldn't spot us. We flew good formation and as we approached France we started climbing. We got up to 11,000 feet and put ourselves in echelon and then started our evasive action. We all expected plenty of flak because we knew that the radar station was well protected. You could tell that everyone was nervous by the way they flew their airplanes. I flicked on my bomb arming switch as the first flight dove on the target. It was a beautiful sight to see. I was in the last flight down and was able to see the other boys go down as I started my dive. Everyone went straight down and they all pulled streamers because of the speed we built up in the dive.

As I went down, it looked like hell below me. There were at least four ships in the dive all the time and every one was firing his guns all the way down.

As I went down I saw a lot of bomb burst in the water. There were also plenty of them on the station. I pulled out at 4,000 feet and kept going down toward the deck away from land. As I was catching up with my flight, someone called out 'bogies at 4 o'clock." I looked all over the sky but couldn't see a thing but our airplanes.

We reformed nicely and had a good formation all the way home. We landed at 1945 giving us a three hour mission and my ass was really sore. The Red Cross gal was waiting with coffee and doughnuts, thank God. We all needed it. Everyone was jubilant over the success of our mission.

I have to get up at 0430 for our first mission tomorrow. Something big is coming off very soon because all our targets are in France along the coast near Marseilles. I hope it's the blow to end the war.

Saturday, August 12

Was awakened at 0445 because I was on the first mission. It is an eight ship mission and we were to bomb gun emplacement at Savona, Italy. We took off at 0620 and reached the target at 0705. As soon as we got near Savona, they started throwing flak at us. We took evasive action and got into echelon. The flak was behind us at first and then they were shooting ahead of us, but as we started to peel off they got our range but good.

I heard an explosion and felt my plane jump and I knew I had been hit. It wasn't serious though and as soon as I felt that everything was OK I got mad. I dove on the target cursing the Jerries all the way down.

I could see their machine guns on the ground shoot at me so I fired my guns all the way down. I must have hit them because before I let my bombs go, they stopped firing. Let go the bombs and began weaving over the water.

One of our boys, Lussier one of the newer pilots, had been hit and he was ahead of me. His plane was smoking like hell. He had to bail out about five miles from land. We circled over him as long as we could and then just made it back to the base on what gas we had left. We had called Blacktop (our radar station) and given them a fix on him and they sent out the sea air rescue party. We landed at 0820, and as we landed another flight was taking off to cover Lussier until the rescue party came. They sent flights out today, each one covering him all day until he was finally picked up by the rescue launch.

I'm in a big mission this afternoon and we are going after a big railroad terminal and yard below Marseilles. It's a 36 ship mission and there are 12 ships from each squadron in the group. We were briefed and then we went out to our planes. The 522nd took off first and the 523rd followed them. We were last off at 1645. Each squadron got into formation. We met at the tip of Corsica and then headed for France. We carried belly tanks, but this was such a long mission we had to take it easy to conserve gas.

We hit the French Coast right on the dot and then swung inland so that we would avoid the heavy flak areas. We got near the target and went into echelon. Each squadron had a certain part of the yard to hit. Our target was the end of the yard. We had to bomb two tracks leading out so that we could block up our end. One squadron took the other end and the third squadron hit the middle of the yard. They really threw hell at us. Flak was thick enough to walk on but their aim was piss poor.

We peeled off on the target. I was the tenth man down and I saw the bombs hitting right smack in the middle of the tracks.. I fired my guns most of the way down at some boxcars , let my bombs go and pulled up weaving like hell and started back to formation. Someone called out some bandits coming up behind and below us but by the time we swung to meet them they took off. One of the boys in my flight shot down one of them, an ME 109 (a German Fighter plane) and a fellow in the other squadron got another one.

When the bandits were first called out, I felt as if a hand was squeezing my heart, but the feeling of fear passed quickly and I actually wanted to get into a fight. We had them way outnumbered and we had plenty of firepower to give them. They ran fast and we reformed and went home. Two of our boys had to land at the other end of Corsica because they were low on gas. I finally landed and still had 100 gallons of gas left. We were interrogated and then went to supper which was a swell meatloaf meal for a change. We had a big bull session that night about the mission and we really had a good time. Drank beer and laughed at how we gave the Jerries hell.

Our advance echelon is leaving here in the morning which means that another invasion is on its way and we'll be moving very soon. I'll bet it's the Marseille area because that's where all of our targets have been the last few days.

Sunday, August 13

Doc drove a bunch of us to Bastia. As we were leaving, we saw a General's car coming into our area. He came on an inspection tour. The invasion is coming any day now, because we have been alerted. Groups of us take turns sitting near our airplanes so that we can take off at a moment's notice.

Invasion

Monday, August 14

Got three letters and was tickled to read that the folks finally got some mail from me. Had supper and listened to the radio till 2000 when we had a meeting of the whole group in front of the Officers Club. This is it. The invasion of Marseilles area started at 2000 tonight but the major landings are to take place tomorrow from 0800 on. When it was announced, I felt a shiver of joy. This is the big show to end the war and we are going to play a big part in it.

There are going to be concentrated landings along about 70 miles of coastline between Toulon and Marseilles and there are also going to be diversionary thrusts at Genoa at the French-Spanish border. C 47s are going to drop 500 dummy parachutes to make Jerry think we are coming in there. The main thrust still comes in at Marseilles. The Navy is using a new weapon called "The Drone.". They are radio controlled landing boats that come up on the beaches and then explode. They will facilitate the clearing of the mines.

The air cover is going to be tremendous and that's where we come in. Beginning at 0500 tomorrow morning we have gun positions along the landing beaches to bomb and we must be through by 0800 when the first wave of troops go in. Everything is timed to the minute and we are going to have flights taking off every 15 minutes all day long. That is going to go on all day at every base in the three Air Forces taking part.

There will also be three aircraft carriers which are going to keep 200 planes in the air all day over the beachhead

We had a special briefing of all pilots after the meeting and our group is going to be the first one to bomb the beachhead. The sky will be full of planes tomorrow so we were shown which air lanes we are to use. It's going to be a big and wonderful show and it's sure to end the war very soon. Came back and had a snack, saw some training films and then hit the sack. We are going to need all the rest we can get in the next few days.

Tuesday, August 15
D Day for the Invasion of Southern France

I was not on the first mission so I woke at 7:00 and had breakfast. Went down to the line and took part in a mission that Col. Mack is leading. We will take off at 12:05. Came back and played Solitaire for awhile and then checked the news on the landing. It seems we've taken the Germans completely by surprise or else they don't have the men, but our landings are going on without any opposition at all and are being joined by French Partisans. The landings all came off as planned and some were even more successful.

Went to the ready tent at 10:30 and was briefed. We are going after two strong points on the coast. Our timing has to be perfect because two minutes after we bomb, assault troops are going to take the beaches. Came back and had lunch and then went to our planes. We were warmed up and waiting to go at 12:00. Take off was OK and we headed for the target. We are carrying 1,000 lb. bombs which make the plane fly like a ton of shit. We neared the target ahead of schedule so we had to circle for awhile. Dropped our bombs and called the control station that had been on the beach after the first landing and they told us everything was OK. Headed home, landed and was briefed.

Wednesday, August 16

I'm not on any missions today, so Neilson and I went to Bastia. Special Services got a new stock of pocket books in so we took enough to keep us busy for a week. Got a big load of mail today and was tickled. Read and reread the letters. You'd never know that an invasion was going on near here because everything is so peaceful and quiet. The news is still good and everything is going as planned.

Thursday, August 17

I'm on a mission that's being led by the Colonel. It's an armed recon over France. We're carrying wing tanks and plenty of ammunition. We are just going out to fly over France and look for stuff to shoot up. We took off at 1030 and flew to France. We started patrolling and didn't see a darn thing. Suddenly the Jerries started shooting at us, but the flak bursts were low and behind us. We took evasive action and about half an hour later we got some more flak. No one was hit.   I think the Jerries just shoot to give themselves confidence.

The mission was very uneventful. There were no trucks or troops in sight and we were all itching to go down and strafe. Landed at 1330. Today's mission was my eighth and it was piss poor. Better luck tomorrow I hope. We did fly good formation today. Even the Colonel noticed it and commended us on it. Reasman got back from the hospital today and he looks good.

Friday, August 18

Took off at 1115. I was flying as Mosher's (one of the senior pilots) wing man and for a guy who has had as much time in combat as he has, he stinks.

His flying is best described as "erratic which made staying in formation difficult. My engine cut out as we were going up to France but it caught up as I switched gas tanks. Had to really push my plane to catch up.

Our mission was a patrol over the beachhead and it was very uneventful as far as we were concerned. One of the pilots had been forced down so we went down to cover him until help came. My gas was getting very low so we had to head home. I landed with only 30 gallons left. My tail wheel wouldn't unlock and the runway was too slippery to use brakes so I had to ground loop at the end of the runway to keep from running off. No damage to the plane or this pilot.

Saturday, August 19

Today is one of those rest days for me. After supper eight of us piled into a command car and set off to go swimming. We took a very wild drive down to the beach. We parked near where an LST (Landing Craft) was partly sunk. We swam out to it, about half a mile offshore and we explored it. We found cases full of 20mm shells so we took a case and floated it back to shore.

Started back to camp and saw a sow with ten little piglets. The boys stopped to try to catch the pigs. They were fast as hell, but we finally caught two of them. Got back to camp and took the pigs to the Officers Club where they made a big hit.

Sunday, August 20

We were briefed for our mission at 0945. It's another patrol and we took off at 1030 and flew to the Toulon area. We had a strip of land about 30 miles square to patrol

We practiced breaks the whole time. My engine has been burning a lot of gas and running a little rough so we took it easy going home but I landed OK. About 1600 we drove down to the beach and stayed there for 1 1/2 hours just lazing around in the nice white sand and swimming in the cool, calm Mediterranean. I love this life. I don't see how I'll be able to go back to a regular job when the war ends.

Monday, August 21

Didn't have a mission yet today so I read all morning and then went to have lunch. One of the boys, Neal, one of the new pilots, was shot down today but he ditched his plane in Genoa Harbor and he was picked up 1 1/2 hours later. They haven't lost a man in a long time. Went to supper at 1730. We had a patrol mission which takes off at 1845. I found out today that I've been credited with 12 missions. I thought I only had 10. Well, I'm certainly not going to argue about that.

We took off at 1845 and flew to France. Two of our men had to turn back, so we only had a six man patrol. Flew our patrol until 2115 and all we saw was a couple of English Spitfires. It was dark when we started back and believe me, it was really black. I couldn't help but being scared. We got lost coming home and Blacktop (the radar guys who track us) brought us right over our field. It's a good thing we had plenty of gas.

Tuesday, August 22

At 1000 we were briefed on our mission. Our target is a road leading out of Turin, Italy. We have to block the road and to fly armed recon on the way back. We took off at 1045 and picked up a course to Italy.

One of the boys had to turn back because his belly tank wasn't working. We got to our target and bombed at 1200. Our flight got four direct hits out of six bombs which is darn good bombing. There was no flak at all so we circled and got a good look at the road. It was really clobbered.

We climbed to 6000 feet and looked over a couple of airfields for a target to strafe. They were deserted, but as we pulled over them we spotted a train of about 30 boxcars. We peeled off on it and strafed it from one end to the other. When we pulled up the locomotive was all busted up. Steam was pouring out of it and two boxcars were blazing. We really did a job on that train. As we pulled up, we saw another train pulling into a station about five miles down the line. We peeled off on that baby and really poured the slugs into it also. It was a locomotive, two passenger cars and three boxcars. Off on a siding were six more boxcars which we sprayed also.

We pulled up and decided to make another pass at it, so down we went again. On my way down I poured a lot of slugs into a big building right next to the station, and then I pulled my pipper (sighting device) up on the station and just held the trigger down and poured slugs into the station.

Then I pulled the pipper up on the boxcars on the siding and went right up the line throwing bullets into them. I could see my tracers pouring into them. Pulled up and not a shot had been fired at us so we circled and went in once more. The locomotive was all busted up, two boxcars were smoking and one end of the station was burning. We sprayed it very liberally again and then headed for home.

That was the most fun we have had in a long time. It really is a thrill to skim over the ground and watch your bullets tear into the enemy.

Got back at 1315 and had lunch. We were credited with two locomotives, four boxcars and a railroad station. That's a good score for three hours work.

We are moving from here to Southern France at the end of this week. That's going to be a good deal. We can't wait to get there.

Wednesday, August 23

We had a pilots meeting. It was the usual stuff: cut the radio chatter, be careful about landings and other poop which we have had time and time again. While we were at the line a call came in for them to send a 12 ship mission on an armed recce to the Po Valley. I was on it so a bunch of us beat it back to our tents to get our guns and then we went back to the line.

We were briefed at 1415 and took off at 1500. We formed up and flew to Italy, entering the coast near Savona. The country around there is very mountainous so we stayed up around 12,000 and started our recce.

Sweeney (one of the senior pilots) was leading the flight and I don't think he knew what he was doing because we hardly went near the Po Valley at all. It seemed that we were flying aimlessly around the mountains. We saw a bunch of four motor transports on the road and we started down to bomb them but they all had big white stars (identity for allied troops) on them so we pulled up.

We knew that we were near our lines in Southern France then and our gas was getting low so we headed for home.We jettisoned our bombs in the mountains and made an uneventful trip back.

It is too bad that it was a wasted mission because when a call comes the way it did, that usually means that there was enemy activity and there could have been good targets for us.

Got back at 1800. Had supper and went swimming. Got back about 2000 and was tickled pink to find Dick waiting for us. He had driven down from his field. I didn't realize how much I missed him until I saw him. He cracked up on take-off on his first mission and got a scratch so he got the Purple Heart. The poor guy is P.O.d and miserable. He doesn't like his outfit or the fellows in it and misses us. He's moving in a couple of days also and we are all going to France, so we're hoping to get near enough to see each other.

Thursday, August 24

The news is marvelous and we all are hoping that the war will be over by Christmas. I caught a ride to Bastia. When we got to town, there was a holiday mood in the air. Paris was liberated last night and most of the people on the island are French so they had good reason to celebrate. All the sidewalk cafes were jammed and French flags were everywhere.

Caught a lift back to camp and then started packing my stuff, for tomorrow we go to France. Lafayette we are here. We're going to fly over to an airfield that has already been prepared for us by our advance detail.

We are all anxious to get to France. Things should be pretty nice over there. We are supposed to move into an old German airfield that has three big hangers on it, and they are all intact. We've seen the place from the air a number of times and it looks good.

I got a letter from Judy, home and by brother Morty tonight. The kid wrote a nice cheerful letter.

I hope he goes to radar school because it would be swell training for him. Judy's letter was, as usual, cheerful and it made me feel really good. This war is fun now that we are winning.

France

Friday, August 25

We finally went down to the line to wait for the A-20 which was flying us to France. We had to wait until 1200. While waiting, I wandered around the forests and found lots of grapes and pear trees. Ate my fill of them and then took a couple of pears for later. We finally got on the A-20 which is built to carry four men and we had eight. We made the trip OK and finally landed at Le Luc Airport at 1245.

This airport is a tremendous field surrounded by mountains. The field has been leveled and it's pretty good but twice as dusty as Corsica if that is possible,

We ate a meager lunch of Spam, C ration biscuits and tomatoes and then they took us to our quarters. They are about two miles up the road from the field. Our squadron has taken over a nice villa with lots of houses around it. I got a little two room house across the road from the villa which I share with Reece, Reasman and two other boys. Being as I was the first one to find the house, I got myself a nice spot near the window.

The Germans must have been living in this villa before we got here and from the look of things, they must have been pigs. Every room was filthy. The tables, chairs and closets were all very clumsily made.

The Jerries must have left in a hurry because they left stuff lying all over the place. We found 50 cases of German machine gun bullets and loads of equipment. I got a Jerrie gas mask which is practically brand new.

The boys found a wine cellar and we shot the lock off the door. Each man took a bottle of what tasted like vermouth. The colonel got very P.O'd and ordered it all put back. Most of the boys put it back and then took it again later.

Spent the rest of the afternoon looking through the villa. The French people who owned it were very modern. They had electric lights in all rooms, beautiful flower and vegetable gardens with modern farm machinery. They even had their own garage and machine shop. I played with the lathe and got a kick out of it because it reminded me of my days learning to be a tool and die maker. Walked down the road and at the next house found a well that had the coolest and most delicious water we've had in a long time. We had supper at 1730 and then we drove down to the local swimming hole. It's a beautiful stream with the water running through it very fast which helps to keep it clean. We all had to wear underwear pants because the locals swim here also. The water is very cold but you feel really refreshed after swimming.

Stopped in town and had a glass of vermouth which was pretty good and talked to some people. We gave them cigarettes and gave the kids candy. There was one little girl about nine years old who was the cutest little thing. I gave her a roll of life savers and some chewing gum. It's a pleasure to go anywhere around here. The people and the country are clean and everyone is glad to see us. They all wave a smile at us. When they found out we were fliers everyone and his cousin came over to look at us. It felt good being made a fuss over for a change.

Came back to our houses and we swept ours out and set up our cots. We got a table and a couple of clothes closets that the Germans had left and we were pretty well set. We hit the sack. Before I fell asleep, we heard a lot of rustling noises. The next AM we found a chocolate bar nibbled into by mice. When we first got here, I didn't like the place that much, but now that we're settled, it's fine.

Saturday, August 26

On the first mission today and we took off at 0750 and bombed a bridge and road near the Rhone River. We had a slight overcast to fly through but it was a pleasure flying without the belly tanks on the plane. Coming back we got lost and flew over Marseilles. All of a sudden there was flak all around us. We couldn't figure out because Marseilles was supposed to have been taken two days ago. We didn't stop to figure it out and we immediately took violent evasive action. One of our boys got a flak hole in his wing, but that was all.

We landed at about 1100 and then had a pilot's meeting. We were told that anyone caught looting anything will be court marshaled. Major Andres then asked who it was that exploded a hand grenade near the area yesterday and one of the boys confessed. Then he asked who shot the lock off the wine cellar. I was one of them, so I fessed up. He didn't say anything, but we are having a meeting tonight with the Colonel and I hope we're not in for any trouble.

After chow went swimming. Tonight we weren't even embarrassed about swimming in our underwear shorts. The water was cold as usual but very refreshing.

The people still wave as we drive past. Doc told us that whenever a place is liberated, the first day the people throw their arms around you; the second day they wave and smile; the third day they are so used to you they ignore you; and the fourth day the prices go up.

Came back from swimming and got our beer ration of six bottles, and then went to the well to try to cool them off but we had that meeting at 2000 so all we could do was get them slightly cool. Waited for half an hour for Colonel Mack but he didn't show up, so the meeting was called off.

Today's been a funny day. I've felt sad all day and my thoughts have been of home. I wish I had Judy's picture here. That would help. I know it would.

Sunday, August 27

I was on the second mission of the day and our target was a road near the Rhone River. At 1100 the mission was called off because of an accident on the runway. Had chow and then we were briefed and taxied out for takeoff. We are only carrying belly tanks this time and our mission is to strafe targets of opportunity on a road running along the Rhone River.

We had to sit on the runway for 20 minutes because some Joe dropped his bombs on the runway while taking off. Luckily they didn't explode.

We took off at about 1900 and climbed to get altitude all the way until we reached Avignon. We dropped our belly tanks and peeled off on the road.

We went down in sort of a string echelon so that we could get maximum coverage of the road. There were a lot of German tanks and trucks which we shot the hell out of. When we pulled up, we had left three tanks destroyed, two trucks burning and Germans running for cover.

We got a lot of small arms firing and as we came off the target, my plane bucked and I heard an explosion that sounded like metal tearing. I thought I had it but everything seemed OK so I kept on going. We kept weaving across the road for about 20 miles diving on trucks and tanks and strafing everything in sight. They were shooting at us all the way but it didn't bother us much. It's funny but I could see tracers coming up at me and flak bursting near me and yet it didn't scare me at all. On missions like this you really feel you are fighting the war.

As we reached the end of the road, we pulled up and off to our left we saw a big airfield with about thirty planes on it all lined up in nice rows. Perfect for strafing. It looked too much like a set up, but we were feeling good, so we dove on it anyway. Sure enough, it was a trap, because they threw everything plus the kitchen sink at us. The planes must have been dummies, because we poured enough bullets into them to blow up the whole country and they didn't even burn or smoke.

We pulled off that field but fast and I did things with my P 47 that I never dreamed could be done with my plane. We had to take very violent evasive action and I was throwing the poor plane all over the sky. Half the time I had it over on its back and on its side. I think we were flying at about 300 mph most of the time, but I couldn't swear to it. When you go down on a target, you don't have time to watch your instruments. You fly by where your bullets go and by the seat of your pants.

We turned around and headed back down the river looking for more targets on the way home. We dove on two German trucks and the bastards tried to fool us by lighting a yellow flare which is supposed to mean that they are friendly. They haven't heard about all of our trucks having white sheets on the tops. When we pulled off, we left two burning trucks and plenty of dead Jerries. We drew plenty of flak and small arms fire all the way down the river, but no one was hit and finally we pulled up to about 9,000 feet, reformed and headed home. We landed just as darkness was setting in.

Monday, August 28

Not scheduled for a mission today so I went to the line to have the life raft taken off my parachute now that we will be flying over land all the time. Today was a nice lazy day. We heard Mosher was shot down today by small arms fire, but they think he is OK.

Tuesday, August 29

Heard that a lot of mail had come in so I went to the flight line to see if I got any. No luck, but when I got back there were two letters on my bunk. Lunch and then to the flight line for a mission.

Our mission is another armed recee over the Rhone River and I must say that I'm leery of it. Mosher was shot down yesterday but he got out OK. We took off at 1330 and flew to the Rhone Valley. As we got over our recce area my plane started throwing oil over the windshield. We dove on a couple of trucks and I couldn't see through my gunsight and had to fly where my tracers were going. I pulled up and called the flight leader and told him I was going home. He gave me a heading to fly and I took off.

I must admit I was glad to get out of there because they were really shooting at us. As I pulled away, I heard someone call my flight leader and tell him that the other leader had been hit and bailed out. I picked up my heading and climbed like hell to get over some high mountains ahead of me. The weather wasn't good and I got off course and ended up out on the coast near Marseilles. I called "Baggage" (the radar control) and he gave me a homing which I flew for awhile.. He kept calling me and telling me where I was all the time. I missed seeing the field the first time I tried for it so Baggage gave me another homing which brought me right to the field. These boys are really good and we thank God every day that they are with us.

I landed OK and came back to the operations tent to wait for my mission to return. When they landed we all were interrogated and found that Neilson had run into trouble and he bailed out of his plane in our side of the lines. He's OK I guess. I'm not ashamed to admit that I'm afraid of these strafing missions now. At first they were fun, but when your friends start getting shot down, it's not so good.

Wednesday, August 30

We're moving to a big field about 15 miles from Marseilles. By 0830 I was ready to go. We reported to our operations tent. I am riding in a command car which is a good deal because it gives us a chance to see the countryside a little. We all hate to leave here because we've got such a nice set-up. We have our fingers crossed about the new place.

The convoy started out at about 0930. Before we left we took any food we could find around the mess area and put it in our car. We stopped along the road and had our canteen filled with some good red wine and we drank wine and ate biscuits, grapes and canned hot dogs the whole trip. We passed through lots of small towns where people turned out in force to wave at us. They threw fruit at us and at one point we bought a couple of melons from a farmer. We really had a swell trip.

We pulled into our new home at about 1300 and this place is a beauty. The field is tremendous and we are going to be the only group in it. This place is called "Ecole de l'Air" and it was once an aviation training school for French cadets. It is in a long, flat valley that is surrounded by low mountains. When the Germans took France, they let the Italians move in with them. The British bombed the hell out of this place. There were 14 hangers on the field, and only about eight of them are useable.

The main building reminds me of the Dewitt Clinton High School in the Bronx where I went to school. It's a long four story building that was bombed quite a bit. Most of the wreckage has been cleared away and we all will live in it.

We have rooms that the cadets used to live in which are really nice. They are about 30 feet long and 15 wide with very high ceilings. The floor is something like marble. There are five of us in each room.

We have all of our offices in the building and the Officers Club is being set up in what was once the library. It must have been a beauty also because there are glass enclosed cases lining all the walls and there is a balcony also with bookcases along all the walls. We have a nice triangular bar in the center of the room the chairs have been taken from all the classrooms and put into the Club and officers Mess. Our Mess is set up in a very large room on the ground floor. The plan is just like a college dormitory except that the rooms are all tremendous. The lecture halls were all curved with seats raised toward the rear. The auditorium is a beaut and we are going to use it for meetings and movies. There are beautiful latrines with showers but we have no running water as yet. It's a shame to see such a beautiful place so beaten up.

Spent the afternoon exploring and picking up odd bits of furniture for our room. We got two clothes closets, lots of chairs, a table and I found a desk about two feet square that I took for myself. Supper was served at 1730 and it was a pleasure to eat at a table out of dishes and cups. Then I spent an hour looking over the wrecked hangers and got a ride to the orderly room and picked up mail. There was really a lot of it, and I hit the jackpot by getting 18 letters- most of them from Judy. I felt as if a rosy glow was on everything. Mail is more important than food. Checked with Group Operations and I'm Airdrome Officer tomorrow.

Thursday, August 31

Took a jeep and went out to the temporary tower which is just a truck with radar equipment. Had a hell of a time finding it because it was still dark out. I was the first one to the truck. Pretty soon the tower operator came and it was starting to get light. The first mission was scheduled to take off at 0630 but they didn't get off the ground until 0700. This Airdrome Officer's job is a racket. I have charge of the tower and direct all traffic on the field. Since we are the only group on the field everything is pretty quiet.

Two French planes and a Hurricane landed here this morning besides one mission and a couple of B-25s that took off. One of the Frenchmen had landed to try to get some gas. Between his French and my English-French mixture, I finally convinced him that we had no extra gas. He took off again, a very disgruntled man. My relief came on at 1230 and I took the jeep to go to eat. I came back after lunch and spent a very uneventful afternoon until I came in for supper.

Chapter 3 – September 1944

Friday, September 1

This building makes us feel as if we are in school again. At 1000 we all went out on the field when air medals were presented to about 30 men. We called it "the junior birdmen's medals." It was a nice sight though and I got a good picture of the whole affair. Later on my way back from supper, everyone was telling me what a load of mail I got, and they weren't kidding. There were 50 letters for me. All the ones that had been missing were there. I was like a kid with a new toy.

Doc Brucker and I drove into town to look around. This was my first chance to see what Salon is really like. It's a nice clean friendly town. There are some beautiful sidewalk cafes with tables set out under the trees. As you walk down the street you cannot help but walk through a bunch of tables on nearly every street. The French are great people.

Saturday, September 2

We took off at 0645 just as it was starting to get light and our mission was an armed recce of all the Jerry escape roads past Lyon. We didn't see a darned thing. Either Jerry is moving at night or else he's ready to give up. In the past week we've destroyed over 2,000 trucks and tanks. The roads around Lyon are littered with Jerry equipment. Landed at 0945 and I now have 17 missions.

We hit some bad weather on our mission and it's finally moving down to our field. It's been raining here since early this afternoon and the wind has been fierce.

We had a meeting today and were told that one man from our group is going to be sent as an aide de camp to a General at 12th Tactical Headquarters and they asked for volunteers. It's a good deal but it means staying overseas for a long time. I was almost tempted to volunteer for it but didn't. It would mean flying twin engine, slow airplanes and that's not for me. Anyway I want to complete my missions and get home.

Sunday, September 3

It is really cold today and the winds are terrific. Went to lunch at noon and found out that Neilson got back OK. I haven't seen him yet but the boys say the Partisans took good care of him.Talked to him this afternoon and everything about his being forced down is so simple. He said that right after he landed farmers came out of the woods and within one hour he was in Partisan hands. They took good care of him and he was with them for three days. He finally saw some American troops. He went to them and they sent him back to our outfit and he's none the worse for his experience. Now he has plenty to tell his children about someday.

I had a mission this afternoon and we took off at 1715. That wind is still terrific. By the time I became airborne, it was drifting off the runway. Once up in the air, everything was fine. Our mission is another armed recce up past Lyon and it is reported that there are German truck convoys moving out of there. We got to Lyon and spotted a small convoy of about eight trucks on the road north of town. We dove on it and I got my first flamer. I shot up a Jerry truck and it was burning before I pulled off. We dove on some more trucks.

We landed back at our field at 2015. Landing in that terrific cross wind was rough but we all got in OK. One of my wing tanks fell off on landing, but no damage was done.

We have all kinds of rumors going around about this group going to the C.B.I. theater. I'm hoping we get go home first.

Monday, September 4

One of the boys met a girl he had a date with and I acted as interpreter for them. I get a big kick out of doing that. My French is greatly improved. Back at camp Doc Brucker introduced me to a visiting Jewish chaplain at lunch. We had a nice talk. He knows Dr. Gordis the rabbi who married my honey and me. He is having services tonight and a discussion on the coming holidays which I'm going to.

Went back from lunch and found that every pilot and every plane is going to be in the air almost all the time today.

It seems that the Jerries are trying to escape in the Lyon area and they are all headed toward Dijon which is about 100 miles north of Lyon. P-47s have been up there all day strafing the retreating columns. Dick's group and ours are having a private show up there. I'm on a mission that takes off at 1630. I was going to ask to be taken off it to go to services, but they need all the pilots today. Anyway I don't want to miss the fun.

We took off at 1630. We are to cover all the roads to Dijon and strafe any columns we see. We arrived at our target area and immediately saw a convoy of about 20 trucks and armored cars. We peeled off on them and must have taken them completely by surprise, because they were just stopping when we dove on them. I picked a nice juicy truck and gave it a short burst, and puff, it burnt like hell. Swung onto another truck and poured lead into it till it started burning also. I caught quite a few Germans in that second one because they were starting to run when I dove on the truck. Strafed them and saw them laying all over the truck and the road.

We pulled off the target and off to our right we saw a five car train. Went over to that and the flight leader got the locomotive and the rest of us set one car on fire and left the rest of them smoking. We pulled up again and about four miles away we spotted about 15 Jerry armored cars trying to beat it through a village. We went after them and got them at a little bend in the road. We strafed straight down the road throwing caution to the wind. A couple of boys got flamers. I took the last four cars and left every one of them smoking.

We pulled up again and immediately spotted this train with about 20 boxcars. Down we went again and we all went for the engine. Two of the boys were really pouring their bullets into it and it exploded before I got there. I started shooting at the boxcars, but I ran out of ammo. That really is a helpless feeling when you pull the trigger and nothing happens.

We pulled up then. Most of us had empty guns and we headed home. Two of our boys were hit but not seriously. They made it back home. That's what it was like on every mission today. The boys say that no sooner did they pull off a target when they'd see another one and down they'd go again.

When we got back and had supper then went to a movie. Before the show started, they announced that our group of three squadrons had set a record today. We got 170 trucks destroyed, 11 locomotives destroyed and three damaged, 70 boxcars destroyed, 90 damaged and countless horse drawn vehicles and horses destroyed. It was a terrific day. The news on all fronts is marvelous., Maybe by the end of September the war will be over. Wishful thinking. I was hoping to be home very soon.

Tuesday, September 5

Met the rabbi who gave me a paper to fill out so that he could mail out New Year's cards for me. Went to a pilot's meeting. It was the usual crap, but one good thing was decided on. Each Flight Leader was given charge of a vehicle for his use and also for his flight. Hunt is my leader (we live in the same room) so we got our car and a bunch of fellows went to town.

Stopped at a small store. For $1.25 I bought three cute silk handkerchiefs and a scarf. At camp I made a package of the silk scarf and handkerchiefs and sent it home. At about 1600 we decided to go to Marseilles. We took our car and we were off. I drove and we got to Marseilles at about 1800. We went to an Officers Mess for supper which was excellent. We had roast beef and soup all served by lovely French waitresses.

The woman who is in charge is an Englishwoman who has lived in Marseilles for 20 years. She came over and talked with us and told us that she has a son our age who was taken by the Germans to work in Germany. He escaped near Dijon and hid out for nearly two years and now he's back with her.

Wednesday, September 6,

Bad weather – lazy day – nothing doing!

Thursday, September 7

We were told to have our baggage ready to go after lunch so everyone started packing furiously. When I finished packing, I put all my bags in the hall to be picked up. After supper five of us caught a lift to Aix, a beautiful town about 35 miles from Salon.

We went to a bar "Le Cheval Blanc" where a young Frenchman, very well dressed, invited us to his house for this evening where he was having a party. He drove us up there in his car and the place was gorgeous--made of stone, all of the floors tiled and very modernistic. We washed up in the bathroom which was comparable to the nicest back home. When we came down, the table was loaded with different kinds of wines, cognac, cakes, nuts and fruit. We drank, talked and danced until 0230 and then caught a ride back to Salon in an open truck. We arrived back half frozen.

Friday, September 8

Was awakened at 0900 for a mission. We took off at 1000 for our new field at Lyon. The field is a madhouse.
C-47s landing constantly. Spitfires are everywhere and P-47s and B-25s are squeezed in also. Before we managed to get off two of us got stuck in the mud and trucks had to haul us out. The weather was awful so we had to stay at about 2000 feet all the time. It was raining and hailing and we kept dodging storms.

At the town of Lure, we saw a railroad yard full of rolling stock. We came over a hill and were on the train before they knew it. The boys left a couple of boxcars smashed and I took aim at the locomotive. I saw my tracers pour into the cab and then -puff- it exploded. That's the first locomotive for me. One of the boys got a hole in his wing from small arms fire, so we took him back to Lyon dodging storms all the way. We left him there and took off for Salon and landed at 1600.

Saturday, September 9

Went to operations to check the missions. As I was coming out the door our God damned Operations told me that I was to stay in Operations all day because I was late for the briefing yesterday.The only reason I was late was because that S.O.B. didn't let us know about the mission until the last minute. There were three of us who had to sit there all day. I was mad I was ready to tear that bastard apart with my bare hands. I've never liked him much anyway. I don't like this damned C.S. outfit either. I did like it when I first got into it and before I got to know what the score was. And that only took a short while. The first chance I get I'm going to get out of this damned outfit. Spent the whole day sitting , reading and playing cards.

One of our boys bailed out on the German border today. It's really getting rough up there.

Sunday, September 10

When I came back from lunch there were seven letters on my bed. One of them contained a picture of Judy. When I opened them and saw Judy's picture a shiver ran down my spine. I didn't realize that I had such a beautiful wife, and when I looked at the picture she seemed to smile at me. I was proud as hell when all the other boys admired it also.

After supper we had a pilot's meeting where we were told that we are going to move in a day or so. I also heard rumors that we may go back to Italy. Who knows? After the meeting a bunch of us walked to town and wandered around for awhile.

Had a drink and then walked back to camp. I'm not used to so much walking and that four mile trip got me pretty tired. Our whole group will stand down tomorrow so that the maintenance work can be done on the planes so that they will be able to move.

Monday, September 11

By 1100 everything was set and we were ready to go. I managed to work my way onto the plane first, a B-25, that was transporting us and took the co-pilot's seat.

The airplane was terrifically overloaded. There were about 16 men and equipment on board. One of the captains from the group was flying it. The name of the plane was "Wevehadit" and a lot of us weren't doubting it much. We took off, or rather staggered off at 1115 and headed for our new field. After we got in the air, the Captain let me fly the plane and it was really fun. The ship handled beautifully.

We got to what we thought was our field in one hour. We unloaded our baggage and the Captain took off again. After he was gone we found out that we were at the wrong field. Our field is about ten miles east. There was nothing to do but wait. Finally the Captain landed again and made arrangements for a truck to take us to our field.

He also brought some horrible news with him. Our other B-25 had crashed and killed Captain Maltby of our squadron and 15 enlisted men. Everyone was stunned by the news and were very quiet for awhile. Everyone of the men on board had been overseas for two years and were due to go home soon. I knew one of the Jewish boys on board and he was a swell fellow. It was a very subdued group that climbed on that truck. No one had much to say when we got to Layette Field which is our new home.

Our new field is set in a valley with a bunch of high mountains on the East side. Captain Malty had come in having trouble with one engine. The field was closed in by fog so he couldn't see the mountains and crashed before anyone knew what was happening.

After we ate, we saw a herd of cows in the field where our tents were, so one of the boys milked one while we all stood about and cheered.

Tuesday, September 12

Now that we're beginning to fly over Germany, we all carry 45's, knives and other odds and ends in case we should get forced down. We took off at 1330 and flew to the German border where we started our recce. We strafed a train in the Ruhr Valley but nothing happened. We were on the deck then and we all narrowly missed some telephone wires. We pulled up into the mountains and started patrolling. We found a couple of trucks and went down and shot them up. They burned and then we started back across the valley. We found another car and truck when we got to the other side and left them burning. Started home and found another couple of trucks and went down and left half of them burning. My gun sight bulb had fallen out and broken so I could only aim by following my tracers.

We finally pulled up and headed home. For the first time since I left Primary Cadet School I got airsick today. I didn't throw up but I felt as if the world was coming to an end. The flight leader told us that we all flew a great mission. I guess I'll have to keep getting sick if he thinks my flying today was good.

Doc Brucker came over and asked me to drive him about 15 miles to a hospital where he could get an infection on his hand taken care of. On the way he told me about the funeral for the men who were killed yesterday. The French people in the town here were wonderful. They gave beautiful spots in their cemetery, they dug the graves, made the coffins, even had the town printer make some paper American flags for the coffins and they all attended the funerals dressed in their Sunday clothes and brought flowers. Doc told me they cried as if it was their own sons who they were burying. The services were very short. Three volleys were fired over the graves and one of the officers made a speech in French thanking the townspeople. There were nearly 500 people there.

Got back at 2115 and found my tent empty. Major Andres ordered all tents dispersed because we are within JU-88 range and they might try to pull a surprise raid on us.

Wednesday, September 13

I have no missions today. Came back and washed up and cleaned up for the first time in two days. Spent the whole afternoon catching up on my correspondence. The weather was miserable all day today and as a result there was no flying. The flak over Germany is pretty intense, but there are so many trains and trucks to get that we are all pretty eager to go on missions.

Thursday, September 14

It's cold and miserable and still raining. Spent the rest of the morning going through and repacking my foot locker and parachute bag.

After lunch we dug a hole in the center of our tent to use as a fireplace and we lugged about six logs to our tent and spent an hour chopping them up. After lunch it cleared up a little and the sun came out so it's been pretty hot all day.

Our mess hall is getting pretty classy with nice metal tables, glasses and glass pitchers. After supper, we went for a walk and passed a small farmhouse.

We saw plenty of chickens, so we went up and asked an old woman standing there if she had any eggs to sell. She gave us six of them. We couldn't make out what she was saying, but we gave her 30 francs which is a little high, but it was worth it.

We walked to this little village and found a small cafe. There was an old man there and he told us that five years ago the Germans came through and shot his son and sent the remainder of the healthy men to labor battalions.

We then came back to our tents to cook our eggs. I poached one and fried the other and they were delicious. After I finished, I lay back on my cot and watched the fire. There was a very peaceful feeling in the tent and I imagine that all the other boys were thinking of home as I was. Jimmy Short, a pilot I remember from Spence Field in Ga. joined the group today and it was good to see him. He's been with the hospital in Naples for 12 days with malaria, but he's O.K. now.

Friday, September 15

No missions today. At a pilot's meeting we were told that transportation will be provided for us to go to Lyon. We were also told to be on the lookout for pro-Nazi Frenchmen around here. We have orders to carry our guns when we leave the base. We also have regular days off from now on. My first day is tomorrow.

Because of a combination of bad weather, the condition of the runway and my illness, I will not fly again until October 8 after we had moved to Italy.

Saturday September 16

We went to Lyon and walked around in the rain. Lyon hasn't been beaten up hardly at all. There are piles of broken glass on the streets but most of the windows have been replaced. It's as busy as New York City. We wandered around town and bought some odds and ends. About 1800 we went into a small cafe and had sandwiches and wine for supper. These loaves of brown bread are about the size of our rolls and about two feet long.

While in Lyon, we saw a lot of F.F.I. (Free French of Interior) men walking around. They impress me as nothing more than a gang of hoodlums heavily armed. They are on the same order as a Hitler Youth organization. They have been robbing gasoline and slugging guards in our camps lately and from now on we carry our guns with us. Most of them are members of the French Communist Party which seems to be running things in France right now. Most of the boys feel they would just as soon shoot them as they would the Nazis and after seeing them, I'm inclined to agree.

Sunday, September 17

Met Doc Brucker and he reminded me that the Jewish holidays start tonight. Time passed so fast that I didn't realize they were here already.

Monday, September 18

After chow, I dressed up and went to Operations to get my pass for the remainder of the Jewish holidays. Caught the command car to town at 1330. Met Reece and we went to meet Doc Brucker who never showed up. We started walking around town window shopping when we met this French fellow and his sister.

They were both charming and spoke English quite well. The people here love to be seen with Americans. I guess it gives them prestige, anyway, we invited them to have a drink with us and they took us to the cafe called "El Baraca". We drank wine and talked. Reece became very infatuated with this fellow's sister who was very cute. He had been studying to be a lawyer before the Germans came and for the past four years he has done nothing because the Germans didn't see fit to let him continue his education. This young fellow invited us to a party at his home this coming Saturday if we are still here. We finally headed toward our hotel at 2330 , and as we were walking down the street, three men suddenly came out of a doorway in front of us. I had my gun out in two seconds, but they just said, "Bon Soir" and we passed on. They were F.F.I. men and lately there have been reports of them robbing U.S, officers.

Tuesday, September 19

I went to the Place de Bellecoeur where I was to meet Doc. The Place is the big square in Lyon and everyone used to promenade there before the war the same as people in the States walk in Central Park. While I was waiting for Doc a Catholic priest came up and started talking to me. I was surprised, because he spoke excellent English.

We talked for an hour, and he told me how happy all the French were to see the Americans. He also showed me a spot on the square where only 3 days before Lyon was liberated the Germans executed five French men for no reason at all.

At 0930 I decided not to wait for Doc any longer and asked the priest if he could give me directions to the Jewish synagogue. He said he would consider it an honor if I would let him take me there, so we started walking.

He showed me the building that had been the Gestapo headquarters and told me that in the basement the Germans had torture chambers and he had seen some of the most fiendish designs for torture imaginable.

We soon arrived at the synagogue and he left. I joined a group of officers from my group and we all went inside. The rabbi was just starting his address as we entered. It was all in French but he spoke so well that I could understand everything he said. The shule had been pretty well beaten up by the Germans. They had torn the altar up and pulled down chandeliers and smashed all the tablets on the walls that were in memory of the dead. The joy of these people is wonderful to see. This was the first Rosh Hashonah in about four years that they could hold services. I got a real thrill out of seeing then so happy.

The rabbi in his speech said they were going to leave the German vandalism as it stood so that people would not forget how they had been oppressed by the Germans. Most of the people were crying, but I think it was more from happiness than it was for sadness of bad memories. It reminded me very much of the holiday services back home.

After the service many came over to us and wished us a happy new year. One old man made us feel as if we were going to break out in tears. He said, "God bless you for making us happy again."

Two young girls and their parents came over to talk with us. The girls spoke English. They said they had been studying English for nearly two years now, because they knew that pretty soon we would be coming. They gave me the address of their uncle in Norfolk, Virginia and asked me to write him a short note and tell him that they were alright. They all want to go to America when the war ends. Over here they think every American is a very rich, glamorous person. I tried to explain that the people back home are the same as they are, but they didn't believe it.

After lunch Reece went to meet his dream girl and Doc and I wandered around town. We went to perfume stores and I bought some perfume for Judy. We were having a wonderful time and we really saw the town. We stopped at a music store because Doc wanted to buy some music. While we were there Doc played the piano. He really plays nicely. After that we stopped at some swanky looking tea shop and had hot chocolate and brown bread and jam. All foods are very high priced here, but luxuries are terrific. At 1600 we met Doc Lowenstein and went back to camp

Wednesday, September 20

I'm a spare on the mission this afternoon so at 1430 I walked down to Operations. The first mission that took off reported very bad weather over the target so we stood down for the rest of the day.

Thursday, September 21

I'm a spare on the first mission if it ever takes off. It started to clear up at about 1130. Was briefed and I taxied out with the boys until they all got off O.K. and then I taxied back. I got a real kick out of being in an airplane again. I wish I could have taken off.

I got some mail today, but being as hungry for mail as I am, four letters weren't enough.   C'est la guerre.

Friday, September 22

We had a pilots meeting at 0830 and the names of the boys who were shot at by the F.F.I. the other night were taken. We were all told to be sure to carry our guns when we left the post. They caught one of our waiters giving gas to two F.F.I. men, so they took the whole bunch to town and threw them in jail.

Saturday, September 23

We were supposed to have a presentation of medals but it was called off because of inclement weather. It's pouring outside and the mud is like glue.

Sunday, September 24

I haven't felt well all day. I can feel a case of G.I.s coming and I've been nauseated all day. I was so cold that I was shivering uncontrollably for about 15 minutes after I got to bed. I didn't feel well at all.

Monday, September 25

Had breakfast and stopped at the dispensary where Doc took my temperature. It was normal, but I felt piss poor so he gave me some medicine and grounded me for the day. I got my own airplane today. Lt. Pribil is going home because his wife is having a baby, so I got his airplane. I wasn't as thrilled as I thought I'd be. I guess it's because I don't feel well. After lunch I read for awhile till I got a headache and had to stop. Today was an awful day for me. My stomach bothered me worse than ever before and I felt as if I was freezing all day.

Tuesday, September 26

I got permission to go to town this afternoon with Doc. A local barber brought me a straight razor that I had asked him to get for me. It was a beauty. He wanted 200 francs, but we finally settled for seven packs of cigarettes. I shaved very carefully and didn't cut myself once. We started preparing to go to town. Doc had stopped at the mess hall and got two loaves of bread, a can of sausages, a can of pork and gravy, corn, pineapple, rice pudding, a pound of coffee, two cans of salmon, and eight eggs we added to the collection. It was quite a package.

We hunted for Reece and he agreed to go to town with us and take us up to see his girl's family. We told him to tell them that we were bringing the makings for a farewell feast and would be honored if they would allow us to use their house to hold the dinner. They own a very large jelly factory and live in a beautiful apartment over the factory. The mother, Madame Moulin was overjoyed at the idea so we left the food with her and went to visit Doc Lowenstein who is in the hospital here in town.

After an hour, we returned to the Moulin house. Reece's girlfriend, Odeile, her brother John and Mrs. Moulin were waiting for us. They made us feel at home immediately. They served the most delicious aperitif I have ever tasted, and we sat around and talked. They all spoke English except Madame Moulin. We finally went to the kitchen and told Mrs. Moulin how all the food was supposed to be prepared. Can you imagine us telling a French woman how to cook.

Finally the call to eat came and we sat down to eat. We had the salmon first on a delicious lettuce salad, and then we had the sausages prepared in a way we never have them in the army with a super French omelet. Then the pork and finally the pudding. We had beer and when we finished cheese and different jelly candies we had the most super delicious champagne. I ate very lightly because of my stomach, but everything was delicious. We sat around and laughed and talked and all got feeling pretty bubbly by the time the second bottle of champagne was gone. It was a marvelous evening and I'm sure they liked us as much as we liked them.

Wednesday, September 27

Spent an awful night due to cramps. I am going to fast all day. That will probably be good for my stomach. Got a package from Judy. Also got an election ballot which I mailed back. Doc came in and we decided to go to town this afternoon. We drove through streets we had not seen before and found a cute little art store that had some beautiful knick knacks for the home. I could picture the women going crazy over them, but they were very expensive and I was broke. We visited Doc Lowenstein for awhile and he is much better. We headed back to camp at 1530.

Thursday, September 28

There is nothing to do so far but General Seville, May be here today to give some medals so we have to be ready for the ceremony. General Seville finally arrived so we all went down to the line to attend the presentation of medals to our heroes. The presentation took over an hour and is a pain in the neck to everyone except the fellows getting the medals. I guess I'll get all excited about it when I'm the one getting the medal.

Thank God my stomach hasn't been too bad today., Maybe it's on the mend. Doc tells me I have a big cavity in one of my upper wisdom teeth,so I'm going to have it pulled one of these days.

This life is getting us all in a very indifferent mood. Moral gets bad that way also.

Friday, September 29

Today is beautiful but cold. I'm not on any missions today so Doc and I decided to pull out my wisdom tooth today. He gave me a couple of drugs to deaden the pain and pulled it out just as simply as I write it here. I hear a C-47 crashed and burned up with a load of our mail on it.

Saturday, September 30

The boys are flying, but I'm grounded because of my tooth. Doc was going in to town in an ambulance to take a shower and then pick up Doc Lowenstein so I went along. We stopped at the Lido baths. For 10 francs you have the use of a private shower room for about 1/2 an hour so I just stood under the hot water until my time was up.

We went to the hospital and picked up Doc Lowenstein. Day after tomorrow is moving day and I'm not sorry. We are supposed to make a brief stop at Salon and then on to Italy. How it will work out, we will have to wait and see. I now have my own airplane, so I'll be flying it on all the moves.

Chapter 4 – October 1944

Sunday, October 1

The weather here has turned from bad to worse and it has started to rain. The rain today has put a crimp in our plans and now we don't think we can leave tomorrow because the planes will not be able to get off. I sure hope we get to leave this hole on schedule.

ITALY

Monday, October 2

I don't know where I'd accumulated so much junk, but Doc took some of it and Reasman took some more because I didn't have room for it. The only ones flying to the new field are those who are flying P-47s over. There is a shortage of transport planes so everyone else is going by truck and boat. We were supposed to fly down to Salon for a few days, but plans were changed suddenly and we are flying straight to Italy. I'm a big shot now with my own airplane so I fly over.

We will not be getting any of our baggage till October 9 so things will be a little rough. Had to repack some of my stuff and put some of my warmer jackets in my bedroll. As I was in the middle of repacking, the men came to take the tent down. There I was packing like mad while the tent came down around my ears, but I continued packing. Gathered up the few odds and ends that I was going to take in my plane. Stopped at Operations and picked up my escape and money kits.

Sat in the plane till 1330 when we finally started up. An eight ship flight took off before us and as we were taxiing to take off when they gave the field a farewell buzz job. We finally took off and I felt very strange after not flying for three weeks. We formed up and swung back and buzzed the field. The clouds were pretty rough so we kept climbing till we had reached 15,000 feet. None of us had any oxygen, and by the time we reached the French Coast, I was kind of dizzy, so I called Hunt and we went down to about 10,000 feet. Finally found our field and landed

We were the first ones in. The name of the place is Tarquina Field and it has a nice concrete runway, but that's about all. The weather is better and colder thank God. Toward evening a bunch of chowhounds (P-47s) landed with our mess kits, sacks and tents. We set the tents up and unpacked our sacks. By that time it was 2000 and chow was ready I was really tired and so hungry that even C ration hash tasted pretty good. There are seven of us in this tent because we only have four tents for nearly 30 men. We will probably have things pretty rough until the rest of our group catches up with us.

Tuesday, October 3

I helped taxi some airplanes to a different part of the field and then came back and started to relax when they called us all to get our airplanes. I went to my plane and we all taxied to our new area at the end of the field. About 1600, they told us that we had to move our tents to the new area. A truck came and we loaded our tent and all our stuff on it, went to the new area which as usual is furthest away from everything. Finished supper as a bunch of C47's started landing, so we had to go down and help unload them. Thank God they had supplies and some more of our crew chiefs on board.

Finally got back to our area and found ten men in my tent. Some of the stinkers we had for Flight leaders had moved in and now that we had more tents they were too lazy to move out. It was too crowded for me and I don't like those fellows anyway, so I moved in with the new boys who are a lot nicer. This damned outfit is all screwed up and there are too many cliques in it. There is no feeling of fellowship that I expected to find in a combat outfit.

Wednesday, October 4

We had one mission today and I wasn't on it. After awhile, I came back to my tent and got my mess kit and went to chow which seems to get worse at each meal.

At 1500 I went to the line to hear the interrogation of our mission which was back. After they were through, I went out to my plane which had been on the mission and hung around talking to the crew chiefs and seeing that everything is O. K..

Thursday, October 5

We have been stood down for the day due to bad weather. After lunch we had a pilots meeting and we were told how rotation of personnel works. We need 100 missions to go home. At the rate we are flying, I'll never get home. Lately I've felt discouraged as hell. The World Series are on the radio now and it's blaring over the whole camp area. It feels good to hear crowds cheering. The war must be very far away for them, and it even seems far away to me.

Friday, October 6

We are stood down all day because of this lousy weather we are having. Rested a little after lunch and then caught a ride into Tarqunia.The town is the same as all Italian towns--beat up and dirty. The people just don't seem to give a damn. Got a haircut and shave for 30 lira. I found a store that sold chocolate ice cream that was made with American ice cream mix and it really was delicious. Finally met my friend and caught a lift back to camp. For supper tonight we had pork chops which even I enjoyed. Fresh meat is pretty much a treat around here.

Saturday, October 7

Went to the flight line. I got there just as the briefing started and I had been taken off the missions. I felt mad as hell, but I've learned to keep my mouth shut. I'm getting so that I don't give a darn whether I fly or not. When the mission got back I listened to the inter-rogation. I've been made Airdrome Officer for two days near the end of the month because I was late this morning.

These boys are all a pretty nice bunch. The only stinkers in this group are the big shots and the Flight Leaders. A lot of them are going home soon and when they leave, things should be getting better. I hope so, because if things don't get better by the time I have 65 missions, I'm going to transfer to the 15th Air Force.

Sunday, October 8

Was awakened at 0530 for a mission. We went to the flight line and were briefed and then went to our ships. Our target is a railroad north of Bologna.
On the way out to take-off position one of my wheels got stuck in a hole, and I nearly didn't get out in time to make it off.

Was the last one off the ground and by the time I got into formation we were headed out on course. We climbed slowly because the weather was stinkin. We dodged clouds all the way up to near Leghorn. By then we couldn't see the ground anymore, and a massive thunderhead was in front of us, so we turned around to go home. We dove for the deck and followed the coastline back to our field. Even on the deck, we went through some small clouds and we all sweated plenty because we couldn't see a darn thing.

Because we didn't reach the bomb line, we are not credited with a mission. It was wonderful flying again. Because I hadn't flown in so long, I really had to work this morning.

Near suppertime a P-51 came over and buzzed us. A P-47 went dashing after him. For half an hour they put on a terrific air show for us. If we go to another theater, I hope they give us P-51s. That's really an airplane.

Monday, October 9

Today is a beauty but the taxiways are so muddy that we can't taxi out so we're grounded. Went to supper but I couldn't eat. I have cramps and fever. It feels like the beginning of the G.I.s again.

Tuesday, October 10

Awakened for a mission. I feel much better today. We were briefed at 0800 and scheduled to take off at 0900, but terrific looking weather has been moving in all morning and by 0900 it was pouring cats and dogs. It was a very violent shower.

Had lunch and then I took off for Tarquina. Still no mail. It seems that no one over here is getting any mail. I think something big is coming off pretty soon. Mail always is held up when something is going on.

Wednesday, October 11

We are on standby for the rest of the day. At 1445 they called us for a mission. We taxied out to take off. On the way out, I ripped a hole in my belly tank and thought I wouldn't be able to take off. Dropped my tank on the ground and took off without it because our mission is only a short one. We are out to bomb a gun position right on the bomb line. As we neared the bomb line, we had to climb to get over some clouds. When we got to the target we had to circle three times before we could pick it out. We dove on it and when we pulled up it looked as if none of our bombs had hit. They shot some 40mm flak at us which wasn't anywhere near us. Went home and landed.

Supper was delicious roast beef. Today was a pretty swell day. Mail would have made it perfect.

Thursday, October 12

I'm not on any missions today. Spent most of the day writing to my honey and sitting out in the sun playing with the pup. After supper we all headed to the show so that we could get seats. The picture was "Mr. Winks Goes to War" which was darn good.

Friday, October 13

At 1000 I was put on a mission in place of some of the boys who are off today. One of our missions took off this morning and one of the boys barely got off the ground when his engine quit on him. He bellied in at the end of the runway and he got out before the plane started to burn.

They brought him back to the Operations tent. He wasn't hurt at all, but I've never seen a fellow so shocked. His face was dead white and his lips were quivering. He got out of the jeep and threw his parachute on the ground and then went behind the Op's tent and cried like a baby. Nobody bothered him and after a while he was O.K..

By then it was time for my briefing so I went into the tent. Today being Friday the 13th has everyone on edge. Flyers are superstitious about little things like that. We took off at 1135 and joined formation. We headed for the target which is a bridge about three miles from Bologna.

Our troops are only a mile from the bridge and it seems that we will screw up Jerries supply system if we knock it out. There were scattered clouds over the target, but we found it O.K. and dove on it. We were up at about 12,000 feet when we started our dive so we went straight down for quite a ways. We only caught a few puffs of 40mm flak which was inaccurate because of our speed in the dive.

None of our bombs hit directly on the bridge, but enough of them hit the approach so as to make the bridge unusable. We joined the formation and headed home landing after two hours.

Saturday, October 14

Our mission is on standby because of bad weather around Bologna. Read until 1500 when flying was called off for the day. We got a command car and went to town and all got shaves. After that we drove to a quartermaster outfit that had showers for officers. There are about eight individual showers with hot water. Boy it was good.

Sunday, October 15

Was awakened at 0700 for a mission. We took off at 0810. Ours is a four ship flight and we have two gun positions to bomb. They are only about 100 yards apart so two men will go after each. When we got to the target area, it was almost completely covered by a layer of stratus cloud which hung at about 4,000 feet. We finally found our target thru a small hole and dove on it. I strafed a house on the way down and finally let my bombs go and pulled up. Jerry put up a barrage of 20mm flak which didn't bother us at all. We returned home and had a nice formation coming over the field.

Came back to the tent and cleaned up and dressed up for my trip to Rome. We piled into a Command Car and took off at 1300. We got to Rome at 1500 and pulled up in front of the Officers Club. The club had been a very snazzy hotel before the war and it must have been a beauty. All the floors and walls are marble and there are easy chairs everywhere. We went down to the snack bar which must have been a cocktail lounge. It rivals many of our lounges back home. We got a booth and had ice cream and delicious cakes.

Lt. Herman and I went up to a private house nearby and rented rooms for tonight, and then we took off to see the city.

We walked to the Coliseum and bought a book of pictures of Rome. While we were buying the book, an elderly gentleman asked if we would like to have him show us around and explain things to us. He showed us so many old buildings and statues that I can't remember them all. He showed us an old church that was a beauty. There was a statue of a little baby that was supposed to bring you luck. All the people who prayed to it and had their prayers answered have left something valuable on the statue. As a result the statue is covered with rings, watches and all such valuables. The priest gave us pictures of the statue to carry for good luck, so we put some money in the collection box. We finally left our guide who was very nice and gave him four packs of cigarettes for which he was very grateful.

We went to the Restaurant Parma which is an Officers mess. The meal was excellent and very well served. We had a Parma cocktail before supper and it was so good we had two more before we finished. It had a three piece band which was " tres jolie" as they say in France. We went to "Broadway Bill's" which is a night club for officers. The place looks like an old wine cellar and is very thick in atmosphere. At midnight the place closed and when we got outside, there was a big brawl going on between paratroopers and air corps who were beating each other up until the M. P.s arrived and broke it up.

The house we're staying in is a very nice place-clean and well kept. My bed was really comfortable. As I started to fall asleep, I heard a scratching noise then whines. I flicked on my cigarette lighter and there was a cute little dog trying to get out of the room. Before I found out what it was, I was pretty scared. When I saw the dog, I laughed to myself and let him out.

Monday, October 16

Paid the woman for the room. It was $2 a piece and well worth it. We walked up to the Red Cross Club and on the way I stopped off and bought a Stars and Stripes. I felt like a civilian going to work in the morning and stopping at the newsstand for a paper. At the club we had a snack and read the paper over our coffee. It was a pleasure, because it was so different from our regular routine and so much like being home again. After lunch I stopped at some sidewalk artist's place, and for $2 he drew a picture of me which was fairly good. Then we went to meet our car and bid a fond farewell to Rome.

Tuesday, October 17

I'm on a mission that takes off at 11:30. Went to the orderly room and got paid $119.75. My total pay is $350 a month now which is not bad at all. Our target is a gun position near Bologna that is almost microscopic. We took off at 11:40 and climbed a little bit to get above the clouds. Half the time I thought I was going to stall out. When we got to the target area it was covered by clouds so we swung over toward the Adriatic. Jerry shot some 88mm at us so we swung over the water and headed home. Landed with our bombs and taxied in. I had a hole in the fuselage near the cockpit where a piece of flak must have hit me and I didn't even know it. I called my plane out for a check because it's using too much gas and that was why I had thought that it was going to stall.

Wednesday, October 18

I went out to my airplane. Spent most of the morning with my crew chief while he fixed up a few things for me. I'm going to spend more time around that plane, because I'm learning quite a bit about it. The weather is beginning to blow up a bit and it's getting colder.

Thursday, October 19

Not much doing this morning but I have a mission this afternoon. We took off at 1400. Our target is a gun position and troop area right on the bomb line and it's really close support work because our troops are supposed to attack right after we bomb. We had to fly along the coast to avoid the clouds and then swing inland. We got some flak near the target, but that didn't bother us. When we got to the target we had to circle while some other outfit bombed and strafed, and then we went in on our target. As we pulled off, the controller called and told us that we had done good bombing which was music to our ears. Came home and landed and after being interrogated, we went to supper.

Friday, October 20

I'm on a mission at 1400, and I'm flying a new P-47, because mine is having some work done on it. Took off at 1415. For the first time since we've been here, there wasn't a cloud in the sky all the way to the target area. Our mission is close support- a gun position right on the bomb line. We got a little flak over the target, but it doesn't bother me any more. Dove on our target and all of our bombs were right in there. With good weather and air support our troops are getting closer to Bologna every day.

Came back and landed. I came in pretty hot and had to ground loop at the end of the runway to prevent running off. No damage. This flying every day is marvelous. Time flies, and everyone's morale is excellent.

Saturday, October 21

My plane is all fixed so I went out to test hop it. Started up and was going to taxi out when my engine started cutting out on me. Shut it off and after having it checked, it was found that the carburator was still no good, so they are going to put in a new one. Went back to Ops and found that I'm on a mission. We briefed at 1000 and started out to our planes when it started raining so they called us back in. We have to stand by, but it's ridiculous because this weather is closing in solid.

Sunday, October 22

Everything is a sea of mud and the weather looks very promising for more mud so we stood down. At 2000 we went for a snack and it started to rain like hell. We dashed into the Club where some of the boys who are going home soon were singing dirty songs. Some of them were really funny. I have a slight sore throat so I hit the sack early

Because of a strep throat which resulted in hospitalization, I was grounded from October 23 until November 2.

Monday, October 23

After chow went to see Doc and have him look at my throat which is pretty sore. He says that I have a minor strep infection and being my temperature is normal, he just gave me some sulferdiazine pills and told me to gargle and he grounded me.

Tuesday, October 24

Doc didn't like the look of my throat so he is sending me to the hospital this afternoon. After chow I went over to Doc's tent to get the ambulance. It took about half an hour to get to the hospital and I felt feverish and dopey when we finally got there. While I was waiting to get checked in an ambulance pulled up outside with a pilot who had crashed while landing at Tarquina. Immediately, everybody started rushing around getting ready for an emergency operation. My stomach turned at the sight of that poor fellow. He was severely burned and smashed up. Nobody seemed to know what outfit he had been from, but later on Doc Brucker told me that it was Foster. He had been in my squadron and I knew him well because we had come to the outfit at the same time. Doc stayed and talked with me for some time and after he left, I had my throat sprayed and my ear checked. About 1800 the nurse came in and I started my pill diet.

Wednesday, October 25

Doc came in and checked my throat this AM and aside from pills, I have to gargle every two hours. There are three Brazilian nurses here who are really a riot. They are always together and they remind me of the Marx Brothers for some reason. Every time I see them coming I have to hold myself back from laughing. My throat feels like hell and I know I have fever.

Thursday, October 26

The Brazilian Trio came in, remade my bed and gave me an alcohol rub that really felt good. A British navy officer shares the room with me with a case of G.I.s.

With all the bridges that have been bombed out around here, they say it takes five hours to get to Tarquina.

Friday, October 27

The nurse talked me into shaving. It was my first shave in five days. The Red Cross lady came in and gave me some cigarettes and promised to bring books and candy tomorrow. My throat is feeling much better and I was able to smoke today without bothering it at all. After looking at my throat this morning, Doc was satisfied with the improvement.

Saturday, October 28

Doc came in and checked my throat and said I may be able to leave in a day or so. My English roommate and I walked over to the Red Cross building and got some more books and gum. After supper we went to the next building where they are having a movie. I like this life of leisure, but I'd like to be back at my outfit. I've been more homesick than usual today.

Sunday, October 29

My English roommate (Harrisford) left today. The doctor came in, checked my throat and said I'm O.K. and can leave tomorrow. At 1600 I went and took a marvelous hot shower in a nice shower room. I wish our outfit would run into a set up like this. Now that I know I'm getting out of here, I'm anxious to get going. I probably have a lot of mail waiting for me at camp. I hope so.

Monday, October 30

It felt funny to be dressed again after six days of lounging around in pajamas. Finally left at about 1030. The bridges around here have all been washed out due to the floods from the heavy rain, and we had to take a cross country route back. To make matters worse, it started to rain again, and when we got back to camp, it was pouring. The boys were glad to see me back. Went down to Tech Supply and drew a winter "Parka", one of those long jackets with a fur hood.

Tuesday, October 31

I went down to the line and went to the paint shop to see about getting Judy's name painted on my plane, but the painter was on his day off so it'll have to wait. Went to calisthenics at 1630. Different fellows in the outfit took turns leading it, and it was more fun than work. The reason we have P.T. is because our dear Colonel got P.O.d because the venereal disease rate in our outfit was too high, so P.T. is a punishment. For every new case of V.D. we have two week of P.T. So far there has been none so our P.T. will end soon.

At 1830 we went to Group Ops to see a training film and get a lecture on "G Suits." A G Suit is a series of diaphragms that covers the legs, belly and stomach and is connected to compressed air in the plane. When we make a sharp turn or pull out, the suit automatically fills up with air and puts pressure on all the lower parts of our body preventing blood from rushing down which, in turn, prevents pilots from blacking out. The suit greatly reduces fatigue. I hope it doesn't reduce fatigue so much that we have to fly more missions before going home.

Chapter 5 – November 1944

Wednesday, November 1

My plane has to be test hopped and I'm P.O.d because I'm still grounded and can't test it myself. My crew chief was waiting for me when I got to the line and we went out to pre-flight the airplane so that one of the boys could take it up for a test hop. Flying was called off before anyone could take it up, but I spent most of the morning out at the plane checking it over with the crew chief. I enjoy working around the plane, and I'm learning an awful lot about it at the same time.

Thursday, November 2

I got six letters from Judy and two from the folks. They were old letters from the last week in September, but they were still letters. I talked Doc into ungrounding me tomorrow so I'll be able to take my plane on a test hop and wing it out a little. It's my first chance in weeks, and I can't wait.

Friday, November 3

The group was stood down today because of bad weather over the target. I got five more letters from Judy today. All of them were from the beginning of October. Stopped at Group Ops to find out what time the first mission takes off tomorrow, because I'm A.O..

Saturday, November 4

The first mission took off at 0715. The weather is pretty good today so everyone is flying.

We were busy as hell in the tower taking care of heavy air traffic. I handled the radio most of the time and I got a big kick out of handling things. I managed to keep things running smoothly and we took off and landed plenty of planes. At 1000, James, one of the boys, came up to take over for me, because today is my day off. He didn't have to take over. He's just doing it as a favor.

We took off for Rome at about 1130 and got there at about 1320 which was darned good. We got off at the Parma Restaurant and made arrangements to meet the driver tomorrow. We finally left the Parma feeling very good and went to the rest camp billeting office to get a room at the hotel for the night. For $1.50 we got a room for the three of us at the Regina Hotel which is the finest in Rome and is now an Air Corps Rest Camp hotel. Reece and I went to the barber shop and for $1.40 I got the works. My nails are clean for the first time in months. We went to the hotel for dinner. The meal, service and the place itself all reminded me of the Essex House in N.Y. The food was marvelous. They have some wonderful Italian cooks here. After the meal, we walked back down to Broadway Bill's where we drank, danced and made merry.

Sunday, November 5

Dressed and went out and took some pictures and then went to the Red Cross Club where we had some delicious cookies and coffee. Sat there till noon talking with some young captain who was in Rome on a rest leave. He'd been shot down in Northern Italy. It took him four months to get back to our lines with the help of the Partisans. It was quite an experience because he was with them for quite a while and he even went on a few raids with them.

After lunch, we went down to the Red Cross Club to meet our car. Got back to camp at 1645. These days off in Rome are wonderful. We came back tired, but the change even if it's for one day makes us feel good. Living like a human being makes all the difference in the world. Drinking a little, eating good food and being warm and dry does wonders for a man's moral and his health.

Monday, November 6

Was on an early mission today and took off at 0815. Our target is a rail cut about 20 miles past the bomb line. Got halfway up and my plane developed an oil leak so I had to come back. Landed O.K. and was spare on the next mission, but I didn't get off the ground. Went to the line and was briefed for another mission and took off at 1345. Got to the bomb line at 1455 and bombed and strafed a German gun position and command post. All of our bombs hit the area.

I'm getting another damn cold. I've been sneezing all evening and my nose is beginning to run. It's freezing cold here and it's no wonder that most of us have colds. I'm disgusted with everything.

Tuesday, November 7

Our target is a rail cut about 40 miles north of Bologna. As soon as we passed the bomb line, we started to get 88mm flak shot at us and it was accurate as hell. I got a small hole in my right wing which didn't bother me much and had no effect on the plane at all. Flak never bothered me much before, but this darn stuff was too accurate to be ignored. We bombed our target and saw that we had blown up the rail cut so no trains are going to get through and then beat it home.

Wednesday, November 8

Took off at 0700 and I couldn't get my cowl flaps closed so I circled the field and landed. That's two days in a row that I have come back from missions and that doesn't look so good. I'm puzzled because my plane has been checked so many times and the crew chief says everything is O. K.

I'm beginning to wonder if he is not doing his job. I'm on the second mission though. Went up to Doc's tent and got some drops put in my nose. My cold isn't much better today.

We took off at 0840 and headed for our target which is a railroad bridge over to Po River. Got to the Po Valley and found a low layer of cloud covering nearly all of it. Finally found an opening over a town with a railroad yard in it, so we bombed that. As we started into our dive, the flight leader called off a truck convoy that he spotted on a nearby road, so when we came off the target, we swung around and dove on the trucks. We left one truck and one car smoking. Pulled up over the clouds and headed home. That strafing was fun for a change when the results are so good.

As we started letting down when we approached the field, I started getting terrific pains in my ears and sinus. It's from that cold I've got. I really shouldn't be flying, but I hate to miss out on a mission. I have 30 missions. Landed O.K., but my ears and sinus hurt like hell. I'll have to see Doc this afternoon. When I saw Doc Lowenstein, he said my ear was slightly inflamed. He grounded me again and gave me a benzidrine inhaler and some pills.

Thursday, November 9

Went to see Doc this morning My ear still looks a little red and my cold is only slightly improved so he is keeping me grounded. Had a pilot's meeting at 1300. While we had the meeting some of the boys I graduated with came over and buzzed us in P-51s. They were really hot and they came over so low a couple of times that we had to duck.

Friday, November 10

After breakfast, I went to Doc's tent. He checked my ear and said that it was improving. Went to my tent at around 2115 and wrote some letters and got my good clothes ready for tomorrow. I'm going to Rome early in the morning. Because of this darn ear I'm leading a lazy life.

Saturday, November 11

Left camp at about 0830 and arrived in Rome near 1100. Got myself a beautiful room and private shower at the Hotel S avoi-the finest in Rome. Got my pictures that I had taken last week. They were pretty good and I'm having Christmas cards made up with my picture in them. We came across this little Cafe Greco. It was a hangout for Mark Twain, Keats and Shelley when they were in Rome.

We hitched and mostly hiked out to Doc's friend's house. He and seven other officers were living in a 14 room house that was requisitioned for them by the army. The only word to describe the place is "magnificent." Their guest of honor was Margaret Bourke White, the famous "Life" photographer. She thinks she's pretty hot stuff which she isn't. These eight boys have an Italian cook who made a terrific steak and french fried dinner for us. Molte Bono. I returned to the Hotel Savoi at a little before midnight I went to the lounge where they were serving tea and snacks. I ran into my old Flight Surgeon from Goldsboro, N.C. He's with the Air Transport command in Naples.

Sunday, November 12

We hear that our group is restricted to the field by Colonel Nevitt because of the high V.D. rate.

After lunch Reece and I went to see Charlie Chaplain's movie "The Dictator" which is enjoying great popularity in Rome. We had tried to get tickets to the opera, but they were sold out. The picture was just what it was meant to be — slapstick, but I enjoyed it very much and so did the Italians in the theater. After the picture, we stopped at Broadway Bills and danced and drank and finally went to supper.

Monday November 13

Went down to the Red Cross to meet our car. We were hoping it wouldn't be there so we would have to stay in Rome for another day. Left Rome at 1330 and got back to camp at 1530. We were frozen when we got back but the sight of our mail made us forget how cold we were. Went to chow at 1730. What a letdown from the Savoi Hotel. The whole group is restricted to the field because of the high V.D. rate. I think the colonel is a jerk, because restricting the men is no solution to the problem.

Tuesday, November 14

Went down to the line. Censored some mail and then went to the parachute department and got a new oxygen mask and had my parachute fitted with a dingy. Reece and I wandered around the junked airplanes looking for tubing so we can make a gas stove. Found a junk wing and borrowed some wrenches. Then went to work getting the tubing out of it. We had a good time and it reminded me of being back in the machine shop.

We had about four mail calls this evening, and loads of packages are coming in. What a wonderful morale builder mail is. There are joyous shouts all over the area as letters and packages are opened.

Wednesday, November 15

It started to rain pretty hard as we were getting ready to leave the area so we were told to stand by. We went to the motor pool to see about the stove. The fellow who was going to get the parts for us surprised us by having the whole thing finished already. We put our tubing from a gasoline can outside the tent to the stove. Then we connected it to the burner and set the stove pipe up.

At 1900 I went to Jewish Services. Chaplain Honig was conducting the services which lasted about an hour. I enjoyed them and we are going to have them regularly every three weeks.

Thursday, November 16

I was a spare today and as we taxied out one of our planes didn't get off, so I took his place. Our mission is a railroad yard in the mountains north of the Po Valley. We got a little flak while going to the target, but we were looking out for enemy fighters that had been reported in this area. Bombed our target with good results and when we pulled up out of the mountains, over the valley, our number two man, Neilson, got hit by flak and his plane was losing oil. He kept flying along for a while and we thought he might make it back to the bomb line, but he kept losing altitude and finally had to bail out just south of the Po River. We didn't think he would make it back because he's right in the middle of flat land infested with Germans.

We came back, and while we were being interrogated, a British plane that had been circling to land, spun in and hit near the field and exploded. One of our planes had nosed over while taxiing out and the prop was all bent. Today is a bad luck day for this field.

Friday, November 17

Our target today was a railroad line a few miles north of Bologna. We got to the target and dove on it. The first flight pulled right up, but our flight leader kept going down. At first I didn't see what he was going after, but when he started shooting, I saw the boxcars on the track. There was a line of them miles long. More than I'd ever seen before. The fellow in front of me must have hit something, because as I started to pull up, my plane jumped and the air was full of black wreckage. I flew through it and then we climbed "balls out" to get some altitude, because we were right near the mountains. I joined up and came home. I checked my gun camera and I had taken 45 feet of film on that mission. Everyone can't wait to get it developed, because I was the last man down and my pictures should show plenty.

I'm on an early mission tomorrow. A C-47 and a P-47 crashed here near evening and eight people were killed. A Brazilian was in the P-47 and he bailed out O.K. Today has been another bad day for the field. They say that bad luck runs in bunches. Well we've had enough today to last for the rest of the war.

Saturday, November 18

Our target today is the railroad line going north out of the Po valley. It was hazy as hell up in that valley.

We bombed our target, the railroad line, and headed home. No flak at all. The weather has been warm and sunny during the day and cold and clear at night. It's wonderful.

Sunday, November 19

On another early mission. We took off at 0700 and headed out on course. Our target was a railroad line running south from Spezia, but it was covered with clouds so we headed into the Po Valley.

Finally found a hole in the clouds and dived on a road bridge. Our bombing was good. As we headed out of the valley we got some flak, but we all got back O.K. Was interrogated when we landed and then Joe Rothstein told me that I'm a hero. My Air medal finally came through.. I'll probably get the orders in a day or so.

Went to the parachute trailer and got measured for a "G" suit. At about 1600 went for a pilot's meeting. It was more of a discussion of all our flying and gripes. It was darned good. At 1900 we went to see our gun camera pictures of our missions but they hadn't come out very well.

Monday, November 20

After lunch I went out to the tower to take over A.O. for one of the boys who took it for me once before. Stayed there till 1630 and was nearly frozen. After supper I went back to my tent and found mail waiting for me from Judy, the folks and the American Veterans Committee. It seems to have the best ideas of any veterans group that I've heard of. I still feel that the vets of this war should have a strong enough organization so that the government should be forced to listen to what they have to say.

Our restriction is finally lifted so I guess we will start getting days off again.

Tuesday, November 21

Briefed at 1015 for a mission and took off. My tachometer went out on takeoff so I had to land again. The spare took my place and I'm on the next mission.

When I landed, I bounced pretty hard and one of my back wheels came off. The boys tell me that it was skipping down the runway behind me. The next mission is a storage depot at Verona which has the busiest flak in the Po Valley and none of the boys are too eager for it.

We took off at 1350 and climbed like hell until we were at 20,000 feet and on oxygen when we got to the bomb line. Quite a bit of the valley was clouded over, but when we got to the middle, we caught some pretty accurate flak. The clouds were bad also, so our flight leader decided to turn back, and I must admit I wasn't too sorry. I honestly think we could have made it through. We bombed a bridge on the way back and then headed home.

Wednesday, November 22

Today's mission was the same storage depot at Verona. I was spare on the mission, but two of the boys couldn't get off so I took the place of a flight leader. We took off, and didn't get any flak on our way through the valley, but when we got over Verona all hell broke loose. Today, for the first time since I've been overseas, I saw flak that was so thick you could get out and walk on it.

I think we took them by surprise though, because they didn't open up until we were almost ready to dive. We dove and scored quite a few hits on our target.

The flak was thicker every minute. I had my plan all made up to bail out and head for the hills nearby where the partisans were if I got hit. It was a miracle, but we all got off O.K. and had an uneventful ride back across the valley.

One of the new boys was very low on gas, so we left the formation at Pisa and landed at Pontedera. We got our planes gassed up and then we took off, buzzed the field and headed home. Pontedera will be our new field and it has the longest runway I've seen in a long time with all concrete taxi strips. It's an all weather field. We stayed on deck all the way home and when we landed, I found myself on another mission.

After eating, I went back to the line and took off at 1255 and flew up to our target which was a railroad line in the northern end of the Po Valley. Bombed it and got a few hits and returned home. No flak. When we got back and finished our interrogation, I got a jeep and went over to the 319th Service group and took over some laundry and picked up my O.D. uniforms which had been cleaned. At chow Reece and Reasman told me that I really had them scared when I didn't come back with the formation, because they knew it was a pretty rough mission. It made me feel good to know that they were anxious about me. Doc said that he was a little worried also, but he says he sweats me out every day.

Thursday, November 23 - Thanksgiving

At 1600 went to the mess tent for my Thanksgiving dinner. What have I to give thanks for this year? I've got good friends here, but everyone I love is at home.

For some strange reason none of my close friends and I are getting ahead in this outfit. There seems to be a jinx on us. A bunch of guys who came in when we did got their promotions today, but ours didn't come through. They have been leading elements for awhile now, and we are still flying wing. I know that I fly as well as they do, and I haven't done anything wrong since I've been with the group, but yet, I'm not getting anywhere.

We really had a terrific meal today. We started off with soup, then had salad, then turkey with all the trimmings and then mince pie and ice cream. We also had nuts, wine, bread with fresh butter and coffee. I had seconds today on turkey, stuffing and cranberry sauce. We barely staggered away from the table.

Friday, November 24

Went down to the line and got my helmet all rigged up and then checked Op's. I'm on a mission as an element leader, and I felt good seeing that. The weather is pretty bad today, so we are stood down. That means I got the first mission tomorrow and Reece is flying my wing.. Later I went down to the line with Doc Lowenstein and explained the workings of the P-47 and "G" suit to him.

Saturday, November 25

Took off at 0710 for our target which was a rail line in the center of the valley. We climbed like hell to try to get above the clouds, but there was one layer on top of another. We got to the bomb line and tried to find a way through, but it was no go, so we returned home

Sunday, November 26

There is lots of rush and bustle here today because our outfit has twice its usual number of missions. We are expecting a push up the Po Valley pretty soon. Took off at 1215. Our target is a 2,000 man barracks near Milan and we are carrying high explosive bombs. We got up to the bomb line through some really bad weather, but we finally had to turn back. That gave me mission 39.

Joe Rothstein came in and showed me a list of courses the Armed Forces Institute is offering. I think I'm going to put my free time to practical use and take a few of them.

Monday, November 27

It's pouring today, so Reasman and I decided to go to Rome. We left at 0930 and got t o Rome near 1200 soaking wet. Got a room at the Hotel Alexandra which is about the fourth best in Rome. After lunch, I went to the Red Cross Club and got a shave and haircut. After seeing a movie in a beautiful theater, a miniature Music hall, we went to the Hotel Savoi for dinner.

Tuesday, November 28

Reasman and I awoke at 0800 and had breakfast and then went to catch the Red Cross bus to meet the tour of Rome. The tour was whirlwind but it covered everything. The guide was a woman who had been a schoolteacher before the war and she was very interesting and amusing.

We saw ruins in the ancient town of Rome which was built on the seven hills which, in reality are nothing more than slight slopes. We got to the Coliseum, and she told us some interesting stories about it. It could hold 50,000 people, and it had a cover. It would take thousands of slaves to put up the cover. It seems the custom of "Thumbs Up" or "Thumps Down" originated here. When the gladiator had another beaten, he looked to the crowd for a sign to kill the man or let him live.

Next we visited the catacombs which are tunnels that cover 600 miles under Rome. Then we went to Vatican City. St. Peters is magnificent. It was even more beautiful than the stained glass in the Lyon cathedral. Swiss mercenaries were hired to guard it and they did such a good job that they have held their job since then.

At noon we went upstairs for an audience with the Pope. We entered a long hall and the Pope was seated on sort of a throne at the end of it. He just finished a speech he had been making to all the soldiers gathered there, and then he walked among them giving them his blessings. He would ask each one what country he was from. For the Americans, he gave "my very special blessing." The Catholic boys would all kneel and kiss his ring. When he came to me I put my hand out to shake. He looked at me and smiled and shook my hand. We left there soon afterwards, and I must admit that I had been very surprised at it all. The Pope, to everyone in the world, always seemed so high and mighty and inaccessible, and yet we had actually spoken to him. For the Catholic boys, it was the biggest thrill in the world.

We left Vatican City at about 1300 and went back to our hotel for lunch. On the way, our guide told us what Rome was like when the Germans were here. She said that no one used to sleep in their own home because the Germans would come around at night looking for people. Friends used to trade places so when the Germans would come up looking for one man he wouldn't be there.

Wednesday, November 29

At 1330 we met the ambulance and headed back to camp. After a fairly comfortable ride, we arrived there at about 1600.

I was very disappointed to find no mail waiting for me, but everything was in such a hustle that I forgot about mail very quickly. The advanced party was loading up all day and they are leaving for our new field tomorrow.

Thursday, November 30

Went down to the line and saw my plane which had just come back from Naples. Those new bomb racks on it look like canal boats under each wing. Everyone is kidding about carrying a bombardier. At about 2100 word came around that we are leaving tomorrow and we have to be ready at 0715 in the morning.

Chapter 6 – December 1944

Friday, December 1

     Briefed for a mission at 1230 and took off at 1310. I had to put a lot of junk into my plane, because we are landing at our new field. We flew up to the bomb line O.K. and then my plane began losing power and most of the time we were over enemy territory. I was lagging behind even though I had pushed everything forward. We got quite a bit of flak and I got three small holes in my left wing. We bombed a railroad near Parma and then came home. It only took us about ten minutes to get over the mountains and into our field. We are only 20 miles from the front here at Pontedera, the new field. The Appinine Mountains separate us from the front so we should have some nice short missions from here. We landed at our new field and Teetrick (my new crew chief) met me. He had come up with the advance party.

     I was interrogated and then we went up to see our new home. We didn't like it. All of us would rather live in tents. The house is nice, but there are only a few small rooms which the big shots will have and the rest of us are living in one big room with no privacy at all.

Saturday, December 2

     Had a lazy morning because I have an afternoon mission. Our target is a gun position a few miles past the bomb line. We went to take off at 1250 but we had to sit and wait and didn't get off until 1340 because some plane nosed up on the runway. Finally got off and climbed over the mountains. Before we knew it we were over the target area.

From this new field we are really close to the front. We made one circle and bombed it. We had such a steep dive that we built up terrific speed and I had to use two hands and rolled the trim tab back to pull up. The pressure on my body was so great that I passed out for a moment. We caught some light flak, but it was inaccurate. Came back home and our whole mission was only 55 minutes. I hope all our missions are as short as that.

After the interrogation was over, I went to a nearby barber shop for a shave and then went to supper.

Sunday, December 3

It's raining and pretty miserable this morning. After chow, we took the truck down to the line and hung around OP's till around 1000 when we were stood down for the day. At lunch we had a piss poor meal and are all bitching quite a bit about the food. Our cooks ought to be digging ditches or driving trucks instead of cooking. Went to supper at 1700 and heard some ugly rumors that I am going to be Mess Officer because I was bitching about our food.

Monday, December 4

It was cloudy again this morning, so nothing much was doing. I got my application for the Armed Forces Institute, and I'm going to take a course in Feature Writing. Spoke to our OPs officer about going to rest camp this month and he said O.K. I was notified that I am now Assistant Mess Officer because of my bitch about the Mess Hall yesterday. I'm so disgusted with this stinkin group that I don't give a damn what happens around here anymore.

The big joke of the evening was the fact that I became Mess Officer, and I even got to laugh about it after awhile. I was getting drunker and drunker and I was having a wonderful time.

Tuesday, December 5

Went to see Captain Weibert about my duties as Mess Officer. We talked for about an hour about the Mess and the Club and it finally turned out that I'd draw the rations and make up the menus. If I had to fly, the flying will come first. Spent most of the morning hanging around the kitchen and nibbled a little bit. My view of this punishment has changed and I'm think I'm going to enjoy this punishment because I now had a Mess Sgt. and a Jeep at my disposal.

After lunch I went to the line and got briefed for a mission. We took off at 1345 but my belly tank was not working so I had to return to the field.

Wednesday, December 6

Being Mess Officer, I went to the kitchen and got my eggs done just the way I like them. It started to rain, and we were stood down. Went up to the mess hall and checked the rations that we drew for tomorrow. They weren't so hot, so I disguised the sausage by having them ground into patties which should be better. Because I fed the Special Service officer early, I managed to come out a little better than most of the boys. It's still raining like hell outside.

Thursday, December 7

We briefed for a mission up at the Brenner Pass but we were stood down.

Being on the Officers Club and Mess Committee, I went to a meeting at which we discussed the party we are going to have on the 12th to celebrate the group's second anniversary overseas. We made some pretty big plans and it's going to require lots of work.

After the meeting, we were briefed for another mission and then we were stood down again until noon. I went up to the motor pool and made arrangements for a jeep to go to Pisa this afternoon, and then I went back and checked at the Mess Hall.

After chow, we went down to the line and briefed for a Rover Joe mission. Took off at 1400, but we couldn't see Rover Joe because of clouds, so we went into the valley where we saw a hole in the clouds. We caught quite a bit of heavy accurate flak before we finally found a rail line to bomb. Just as we were peeling off to bomb, I got hit and I felt my plane jump about 20 feet. Everything seemed O.K. though so I continued my dive. Then we formed up and went home.

After landing I found five flak holes in my plane. The boys told me that when we started down, I got hit in the belly tank and my gas started spraying out in a white cloud. They thought I had it. One piece of flak ended up in my ammunition box going halfway through a bullet and it's a miracle that the whole works didn't start popping. My crew chief handed it to me as a very nice souvenir from the mission.

Friday, December 8

The fellows on the Club Committee and I took off in a jeep to Pisa to arrange for flowers from a florist there That town is more beaten up than any I've seen yet, but the leaning tower hasn't been touched and it's really an amazing sight because it gives you the impression that it's going to topple any minute.

Then when the flowers were taken care of, we headed for Leghorn. On the way there we passed the food dump that supplies this whole front. Cases of food and stacks of flour and sugar are stacked up as far as the eye can see. It's really an amazing site and it's hard to believe unless you see it. It's more food than I have ever seen.

When we headed for home, it was raining like hell and we got stuck behind a long convoy that was jammed up at a small bridge. We sat there for an hour before we finally moved. Got back to our base in time for supper. Our place is starting to look better every day.

Saturday, December 9

The little Italian boys who clean our room brought us a pretty little table for which we gave them seven packs of cigarettes. Very quiet day with no missions scheduled and there was no mail again today which is discouraging. Joe made some soup tonight so we all had some before we hit the sack at 2300.

Sunday, December 10

After lunch went down to the line. Hung around my plane and kibitzed with Teetrick, my crew chief. At 1500 my plane was ready to be test hopped so I took off. It was wonderful flying alone for a change with no bombs or belly tanks. I climbed to about 10,000 feet and did a loop and a couple of barrel rolls. Checked the plane with full power and gave it a shot of the water to test the super charge and then came into land.

.

Only one flap worked so I had to go around and land without flaps. I got down O.K. and taxied in and spoke to my crew chief about fixing the flap.

Caught the bus and got to the mess hall just in time for chow. After chow we had a meeting of the club committee and got everything ready for the party which is Tuesday. Came back to our room and had a bull session with some of the new pilots. Finally hit the sack at 2300 when the lights went out.

Monday, December 11

Took off at 0830. We had been sweating that mission because we thought it was up to the Brenner Pass, but it was a nice bomb line mission. We found our target and being a little too low to dive bomb, we had to glide bomb it. We caught a lot of inaccurate flak. We had such a nice long glide that we were able to strafe all the way down. Our bombs all hit in the targeted area also. So, all in all, we had a good mission.

The weather turned bad, so we decided to go and take a bath this afternoon. We rode to the natural baths near here, and they really are marvelous. They are naturally heated, volcanic waters and they are just right. I soaked for about half an hour. Had supper and the Colonel gave us a little talk and suggested that we should start dressing up every evening. We wondered why but decided that he's a stupid jerk.

Tuesday, December 12

I went with the ration truck to draw our food and got some extra fruit juice for the party. Finally, I went to this Italian barber in town for a shave. He's a nice guy. There was a little baby there getting a haircut. It was the cutest sight.

After lunch, Joe and I got a jeep and went to pick up the flowers. The florist had done an excellent job making the beautiful corsages. Got through at Pisa and got back to our quarters at 1600. I took my time and really got a kick out of getting all spiffed up. It's the first time since I've been overseas that I've worn my blouse. Joe went to pick up the bus we had borrowed for tonight to pick up the nurses.

We are all pretty proud of our club, and when the nurses walked in, there were exclamations of delight. We had a 20 square foot dance floor in the middle of the room and a fireplace on one side. We had tables arranged around the dance floor night club style, and we had a bar set up along one wall which served only beer and punch. Our painter had painted pictures all around the walls depicting the history of the 27th Group. Everyone raved about them. The pictures showed something funny about every place the group had been in their two years overseas. Over the dance floor, we had a parachute hanging from the ceiling forming a canopy. The bar had been made to resemble a tropical island with a thatched reed cover over it. We also had a lot of easy chairs and couches made, so it's a very comfortable place.

I didn't get much time to visit, because I was busy checking the food, the kitchen and everything in general. I'd get a dance every once in a while, but I didn't see many good dancers tonight. At around 2330 we started serving midnight breakfast which consisted of fresh eggs (a treat for most of our guests), toast, bacon and coffee (which no one drank). The party was a big success.

Wednesday, December 13

Got to OPs and found out that Turner had "bought it" this morning. He got hit in his gas tank and was on his way back to the field when his plane exploded. He didn't have a chance. The boys said they told him to bail out, but he said he thought he could make it back to the field. Went to see Captain Over about sending a cable home and letting the folks know that I'm O.K. because I received a cable from them saying they hadn't had mail in nearly a month. I don't know if the cable will go through, but I tried anyhow.

Thursday December 14

Early mission today. We took off at 0815. After making a few circles of the field, we headed out over the mountains. Our primary target was covered with clouds, so we bombed the first rail bridge that we saw. I saw only one hit on the bridge, but there were a lot of near misses that might have done some damage to the approach. We joined up and headed home. We were over the mountains, and we thought we were over our lines so we stopped our evasive action when all of a sudden "wham" four bursts of flak went off alongside us. We started some violent evasive action and then settled down. One of the boys got a small hole in his tail, but that was all.

Friday, December 15

My plane is in the service group again. I have a new crew chief. My old one was a good guy but a gold brick. I think he might have been overseas too long. I hope this new fellow is an eager beaver.

Washed up and put on clean clothes and a bunch of us went to Pete Turner's funeral. It was a long, cold drive and we were all frozen when we got to the cemetery. We lined up along the grave. The chaplain read the prayers and made a short speech over his remains. The firing squad shot three volleys into the air. One-birth; two-marriage; three-death.

That was the though in my mind as each volley was fired. When they brought out Pete's remains on a stretcher covered with a flag, I could feel more than hear the startled exclamations from the boys. His remains were in a bag which was no bigger than a person's head. The ceremony was very simple and touching.

Saturday, December 16

Took off at 0900. Our target was an occupied area near Bologna, but due to cloud cover we couldn't get in there. We flew around for a while and finally found a hole and went through it to bomb a road bridge. We got one direct hit and some near misses and then we pulled up over the clouds and headed home. No flak the whole mission. Landed and threw the bull with the crew chief for awhile and he told me that he had asked our OPs officer if I could be assigned permanently to that plane. I was glad to hear that, because he's one of the best crew chiefs on the line and he's got a good plane. I hope they do what he asked.

After lunch I moved my stuff downstairs into one of the rooms they built for us. All of the old pilots (that's us now) have rooms downstairs while the new sports are in the big barnlike room upstairs. Reece and I went down to the line to get a stove rigged up. I went to the sheet metal shop where they made me a stove pipe. Then we got a car and took all the stuff to the motor pool to have the welding done. They've started some crap about having to have work orders to do the work for us but they did it anyway.

Sunday, December 17

Went down to OPs but nothing is doing because the weather is bad. Finally went to the motor pool to get my stove finished.

Those stinkin grand officers in our outfit got their stoves fixed first and now the pilots are supposed to get work orders to have theirs made. The sergeant and I get along fine so he helped me and we got the stove nearly done by lunchtime. I really enjoyed working with tools again. After lunch, we went to the 81st and 64th General Hospitals at Leghorn to invite the nurses to our party this coming Friday night. It seems they are having their Christmas party Friday also, so we can't count on many of them.

Monday, December 18

The weather was pretty nasty. I met an engineer lieutenant that I knew and finagled some window panes from him. Reasman and I took the glass back to our room. Spent the rest of the day insulating our room against any drafts. We put weather stripping on all the cracks and nailed blankets up on the walls. Once we get that window put in, we really will be set. Our stove is working fine and really throws off heat. For as long as we are here we are set for winter.

Tuesday, December 19

The weather in the valley is very bad today. I'm not sorry, because I was scheduled for a mission to the Brenner Pass. We finally stood down for the day. Got the carpenter to put a wooden frame in our window for us. He made a perfect fit. Went to lunch at 1230 and then got one of the Italian kids in our mess hall to show me where a glazier lives, and I made arrangements for him to come over and put the panes in for us.. He came at about 1445 and started working on the windows. He really did a swell job and we are pretty well set for the winter. I paid him $2.00 for the job, and he was very satisfied.

Around 2315 some of the boys came in--all a little drunk and before long an argument had started between two of them. One of them is husky and plenty strong while the other is just medium with no suggestion of hidden power. One of the other fellows and myself managed to hold back the rugged individual. Not many of us like the other fellow, but it would have been so unfair for them to fight.

Wednesday, December 20

Our mission was all the way up to the Brenner Pass. As we were taking our chutes out to the planes, we got a call to come back and stand by because of bad weather. Went back to OPs and turned in our escape kits. Doc arranged for Reasman and I to go to rest camp after the first of the year. Got hold of our squadron insignia and took it to a wood worker near here where I'm going to have a plaque made of it. It's going to cost either $10 or two cartons of cigarettes. As far as I'm concerned, it's going to be two cartons of cigarettes. After a movie, Reasman and I took two of the Italian kids who clean up our rooms to their house, because they are afraid to go alone. It seems that the troops around here rob them.

Thursday, December 21

By 0930 we were stood down till noon, so Reasman and I went to the motor pool and got a five gallon can of gas for our stove. At about 1330 we stood down for the day. Came back to our room to find that something was wrong with our stove, so I took it apart, blew out all the gas tubes and then took the valve apart and cleaned it out. Washed the whole works in gasoline and then put it together again and it worked fine.

Friday, December 22

Still lousy weather but we were able to take off at 0815. Our mission was supposed to be a close support one, but the area around Bologna and the front lines had a low layer of clouds over them, so we went further up the valley to bomb a rail bridge. Then we came home. Landed and went to Ops

. When I arrived there, they asked me if I wanted to co-pilot the B-25 down to Naples and Rome. I grabbed the chance, so I gave our intelligence officer a quick briefing of what I saw on the mission.

The first pilot on the B-25 showed me what to do and then we took off. We landed at Rome and let off a few boys who are going to Rest Camp and then we took off for Naples. We landed at Cappochino which I had visited one day when I first came overseas. That place has really changed. They have a really nice mess hall for transient officers and they have improved the field considerably. We had lunch there and then picked up five of our boys who had brought some of our planes down to have rockets installed on them. We took off from Capo at 1430 and arrived back at our field at 1600. On the way, I sat up in the nose and the boys went down to buzz. That was really a thrill, because from the nose it looks a lot lower than you really are.

When we got back, I washed and dressed and rounded up the boys who are going to pick up their dates in the bus. Got to the dance at about 2100. In comparison to our last party, this one wasn't so hot. The crowd was smaller and someone screwed up. We didn't have any flowers or any food. It was a nice party though and finally broke up around 2430.

Saturday, December 23

Our target today is near Bologna, but when we took off and got up there, it was cloud covered over as usual, so we bombed a rail bridge and came home. We got some pretty accurate flak today, and after we landed I saw that I had a hole in my tail.

They were taking the B-25 up for a test hop, so I went along as co-pilot. We barely got off the ground when our airspeed indicator went out and the engine started running rough. I got a little scared for a moment, but we landed O.K.

Sunday, December 24

Nothing much was doing because the weather was closing in. we were finally stood down for the day and we came back to our room at 1000. Tonight is Christmas Eve and because a few lunatics in the world were power mad, here I am, far from everyone I love. Tonight, Judy and I should be celebrating for tomorrow is my honey's birthday. How can anyone expect me to be merciful as far as our enemies are concerned, when they are the ones who are responsible for all this.

Monday, December 25

Judy's birthday. Christmas doesn't mean anything as far as the war is concerned. The weather is pretty good today, so we have plenty of missions scheduled Took off at 1400. Clouds partly obscured the target, but we bombed with good results and came home.

Wrote a letter to Judy. I missed her more today than any other day since I've been gone. Colonel Nevitt announced some promotions and again mine wasn't there. Doc Russell told me that Reasman and I are going to Rest Camp within the next two or three days. That's good news. What the hell is holding up my promotion?

Tuesday, December 26

Doc must have told our Ops Officer that we are going to Rest Camp, because we weren't scheduled for any missions. We went to the orderly Room to get some ribbons for our blouses. Checked on our orders and we are all set to leave at 0930 tomorrow morning.

Wednesday, December 27

We were leaving for Rome at 0930, but our orders weren't ready, so we went down to the pilots meeting. Major Anders told all pilots that he wanted them to stay down at OPs till further notice, because they expected the Germans to try a push on the Italian front pretty soon and they might need extra missions in a hurry. I hope nothing happens till we get back from Rome. I'd hate to miss out on all the fun.

We picked up our orders after the meeting and went out to the B-25 to put our bags on board. We didn't get off till 1015. On the way down, I rode in the nose and took some pictures that I hope come out. We landed at Rome at 1100 and caught a bus into the Rest Camp office and got rooms. Reasman and I have a nice room and bath at the Regina Hotel. Went up to the Red Cross Club and bought tickets for "La Traviata" for tomorrow afternoon. After we took baths, we both got dressed. We wore our blouses and short coats. It feels swell to dress up.

Thursday, December 28

The music for "La Traviata" was beautiful, but I had to laugh when the woman who sang Violeta's part came out. She was as fat as a cow and she looks far from being frail and sick Alfredo and his father were really good, but everyone in the cast overacted. I closed my eyes and really enjoyed the music.

At the end of the first act, we stayed in our seats but wondered where most of the people were hurrying to. When the second act ended, we followed the crowd upstairs where everyone was drinking like mad. We had a Vermouth and wandered into the next room and were amazed to find people dancing to a pretty hot orchestra. No wonder opera is so popular in Italy.

After dinner we went back to a new lounge at the Savoy Hotel and met a couple of fellows we knew. Went back to the Regina at 2330 and met a fellow from the Night Fighter Squadron at our field, a Lt. Gilbert. We sat with him just shooting the bull till about 0115. One of the waitresses brought us some terrific snacks of chicken, so we had a nice time. We were wondering what it was going to be like after the war as far as getting along with other people goes. With any pilot that we meet now, we can always have a good talk, because we all speak the same language. Time will tell.

Friday, December 29

After lunch we met Kramer who invited us up to his place. At 1730 we got to Kramer's office, but he was gone, so we drove out to his house. When we got there, they were lounging in front of the fireplace, so we made ourselves right at home. At 1900 we had supper. They have an old lady keeping house and cooking for them, and she really knows what to do with food. At 2000 Kramer called his car and had us driven back to our hotel. Everything was quiet at our hotel, so we went over to the lounge at the Regina. One of the boys could play the piano, so he beat it out while we all sang.

Saturday, December 30

After lunch we went into the lounge, and I just sat and day dreamed in a nice soft easy chair. I went down to the Red Cross Club and ordered some film for one of the boys. Came back to the hotel and put on my blouse for supper. We had meatballs and spaghetti which was darned good. After dinner we went into the lounge, danced and had a few drinks.

Sunday, December 31

Got down to breakfast at about 0900. Ate and read "Stars and Stripes" over our coffee and then did nothing for the rest of the morning. Spent most of the afternoon in the lounge. Had dinner at 2000 and went across to the Savoy. At midnight, the lights blinked and I'm missing Judy so much that I had to get out of there. Came back to the Regina at 1:30 where the boys were gathered around the piano singing. What a way to spend New Year's Eve.

Identification Photo taken of Lebow upon becoming an Aviation Cadet.

Irwin and his 'bride' Judy on their 1st Anniversary, February 14, 1944. Irwin had just graduated as a Pilot and received his wings.

While on leave in Rome, 'Moose', Lebow, Reasman, and Dewey (from left to right), enjoy a relaxing dinner

Having just returned from mission to his base at Biblis, Germany, Lebow (middle) is seen here talking to a couple of "Brits" who were also based there.

Having just returned from flying the historic Half Million Sortie for the 12th Air Force, Lebow (2nd from right) is greeted by General Cannon (2nd from left). Also on hand to greet Lebow are Col. Nevitt (right) and Col. DuToit (SAAF).

In a ceremony on Memorial Day 2011, in Boynton Beach, FL, Lebow (middle) , along with 20 other World War II Veterans, receives the Legion Of Honor from the Republic Of France.

The American Society of the French Legion of Honor

is proud to recognize

Irwin Lebow

as a Veteran Member
May 29, 2011

Your Dedication and Sacrifice Will Never Be Forgotten

Guy Wildenstein
President

The Legion Of Honor Certificate

Chapter 7 - January 1945

Monday, January 1

Got up late. Finally had dinner at 1330. Lots of Italian delicacies and the main course was turkey with all the trimmings. After dinner, we went to the bar just having a hell of a time. Some fellow came in with a girl who is the best dancer I've ever seen around here, so a bunch of us started to take turns jitterbugging with her. We kept going for about half an hour until we were exhausted. Our whole gang of "Umbriagos" (drunks) is leaving for our respective outfits tomorrow. This place ought to be pretty quiet when we leave.

Tuesday, January 2

After breakfast I phoned our field and made arrangements to meet the B-25 this afternoon. Then Reasman and I went up to say goodbye to Kramer and Kornin. They issued a cordial invitation to come up and see them whenever we came to Rome. We caught a bus out to the airport at 1400, and at 1500 our plane came in. We put our bags on and took off for home. Landed at 1630 and caught a bus up to our quarters. I was tickled pink to find a big stack of mail. I also got one letter back that I had written to Lou Juliano marked "deceased" and I felt pretty bad about it. (When we were in the US and we received our orders, I was assigned to a Fighter Group in Europe and Lou had been assigned to a Flight School in New Mexico.Lou went to our commanding officer and asked to have the orders changed so that he could go into combat and I take his job and he said to the CO that I was married and could stay in the US. They would not change the orders and I later found out that Lou had been killed by a student that flew into him and I was still flying combat missions....Talk about luck)

We had to go back down the line and get new pictures taken for our A.G.O. passes.

Wednesday, January 3

Everyone in this area is on alert because of the push the Germans tried here along the coast, so we all carry guns with us all the time. I'm a spare on an escort mission. Went out to the plane and started up. Everyone got off O.K. so I taxied back in. After putting my chute away I went to lunch. After supper I had to go back to the line and sit through two hours of lectures on the P-47 that we had once before in R.T.U.

Thursday, January 4

Our mission today is a bomb recce of the area northwest of Milan. We took off at 0700 and had to fly over clouds most of the way, but it was clear once we got to the recce area. I spotted a train and called it off because we wanted it in an open area. We let it get to an open stretch of track and then dive bombed it. One of our bombs hit right near the engine and damaged it. We swung around and went to strafe. On the way down, I noticed a big square building with a courtyard in the middle that looked as if it was set up for a motor pool, so on the next pass I went down on the building and set it on fire. We made seven passes on the building and train before our ammo ran out. Joined up and came back to our field. We got credit for one locomotive, two boxcars and one building destroyed and ten boxcars damaged. After lunch Reasman and I went to the squadron dispensary. I have to go back tomorrow to get booster shots for typhus. I don't relish the idea.

Friday, January 5

It was raining today, so there were no missions. Spent the day reading and chatting with the boys.

Saturday, January 6

The weather wasn't so good today, but the first mission got off O.K. I was spare on the second mission. The target was a rail diversion that the Germans had built at the north end of the Po Valley. It's pretty important, because we've been bombing it for the past five days. As we were leaving to go out to our ships a fighter came back with its bombs still on the plane so we were stood by until he could safely land. It was then to late for our mission to take off so the mission was cancelled. Read till near 1700 and then started letters. Doc came over with the news that he has a chance to go home. There isn't anyone in the outfit I would rather see go home than Doc. He has been overseas for so darn long and he's such a swell guy.

Sunday, January 7

Nothing doing again because the weather is so bad. At 1500 I decided to go down and see Doc about looking at my teeth. He wasn't there, so I hung around waiting for him. He finally came in and he was beaming all over because he finally has his orders to go home. I don't blame him. I'm very happy for him, but in a way I'm sorry he's going, because we've become such good friends.

Went to the Club and there was some G.I. in the Club playing the piano and singing songs and he was really good.

Monday, January 8

The weather is bad again today, so no one is flying. At 1330 we went down to the line for a pilots meeting at 1400. The meeting was more of a discussion on tactics and formation flying. The meeting ended at 1500. Went to supper and found out that the Mess Officer is going to the hospital for an operation and I have to take charge until he gets back. Darn it I hope it will not cause me to miss out on some flying.

Tomorrow General Cannon is coming down to present our air medals, so we received instructions on what to do when they are presented.

Tuesday, January 9

On the early mission today. Our target is a division near Citadelea that we have been hitting for over a week now. Part way down the runway my plane wasn't picking up much speed. When I got to the end of the runway I only had 160 mph and I had to pull up to get over some buildings. My airspeed started going down and I just barely made it over town.

By then I was really sweating and my prop seemed to be out, so I came around and called in. Then I came in and landed. When I got back on the ground, I heaved a big sigh of relief, and I found that my prop switch had been in fixed pitch. I felt like kicking myself in the ass, because I hadn't checked it.

Came back to OPs and was given a plane to test hop. I had to wait about 20 minutes till a bunch of planes landed. Then one of them nosed up on the runway, so it was an hour before I got off. Stayed up for 25 minutes and then landed.

After lunch had a talk with the Mess Officer about me taking charge of the Club and Mess for the next month. Got my instructions and went back to my room.

Got dressed up because tonight General Chidlow is going to present medals. Finally at 1900 we lined up to receive our awards. They called us to attention when the General came in and then we stood at parade rest (or a reasonable facsimile) for nearly two hours while they read off all the awards. By the time my turn came, I was glad to just take the medal and get out of there. When the whole works was over, we went to the bar and had a drink to celebrate.

Wednesday, January 10

We've been hitting the rail division at Citadelea for two weeks now. It seems the Germans made it appear we knocked it out in the daytime, but at night they put it to very good use, so it's going to be a daily target for us. We flew up and bombed with good results. On the way back, we saw some boxcars that apparently had been strafed already, but we made a few passes for good measure. I came back to the mess hall and had an early chow. Then took a truck and left for Florence. Stopped at the Finance Office on the way and got the pay for the civilian that's at our mess. We got to Florence at 1430 and picked up the officers whiskey rations. Got back to camp at 1830.

Thursday, January 11

Our target today is a munitions factory at Piacenza. We took off at 0815 and flew out over the mountains. We got about half way there when all of a sudden--whew--flak was bursting all around us. We really did some violent evasive action till we got out of that area. We got to our target and peeled off on it. They sent up a barrage of flak and I got hit again, but everything seemed O.K. so I continued my dive. We scored nearly all direct hits on the main building of the factory, and the next flight up there after us reported fires burning when they got there.

We came home and when we landed, I found 18 holes in my ship. I really got it this morning. Went to lunch and then back down to Ops because I was on another mission. We took off at 1400. Our target was a railroad area off the Brenner Pass rail line and it turned out to be a milk run. We didn't see any flak, and we got back at 1630.

Friday, January 12

Went to communications to check out the radio we bought. While I was there, I arranged to get fire extinguishers for our mess and picked up a piano tuner. Came back to the mess hall and collected a few delinquent bills from the pilots. After lunch we took off for Leghorn. Stopped at the 12th General Hospital to see Moose. He's getting along fine and expects to get out in a few days.

I went to the shoe salvage dump to try to get shoes for all the Italians that are working around the kitchen. Have to have requisitions. Damn the Army red tape. There were loads of shoes that were partly worn and no good for the troops. The Italians would love them.

After supper I had to stay at the club and get the place set up for the party. At 2000 the band came and at 2030, the fellows and girls started arriving. The party turned out to be a pretty quiet affair.

Saturday, January 13

It's raining slightly and lots of low clouds so we were stood down for the day. At 1900 they showed some gun camera films in the club and at 2000 they showed the movie "Double Indemnity."

Sunday, January 14

We were stood down all day because of bad weather, so we had a pilots meeting this morning. It was just the usual "poop from group". Our intelligence officer gave us a good talk, and then I talked to the boys about the club and mess and told them to bring any suggestions they might have for improvements.

I spent most of the afternoon reading a mystery story and playing with the tremendous white dog we have. He really is big and is the friendliest dog I've ever seen. Made arrangements to go to Florence on Wednesday.

Monday, January 15

My mission doesn't take off till 1130. Our target was above the Adriatic in the extreme Northern end of the valley, so we were over water most of the way. We made it to a rail cut and then strafed the rail yard. We also made one pass over what had been an enemy airfield, but it looked pretty deserted so there was no action.

Tuesday, January 16

The Mess Sergeant told me the Italian boys who have been working in the mess hall have been helping themselves to supplies from the kitchen. I'm going to have a meeting today and lay the law down. Had lunch at noon and then took off for Leghorn. Dropped a sergeant at the hospital and went to the Quartermaster Depot, but with my requisition and my trying to talk them into it, I still couldn't get shoes for the Italians. At 1830 we had a meeting of the Club Committee with plans for the dance this week.

Wednesday, January 17

The sergeant and I arrived in Florence about 1230. We spent the afternoon shopping around. We found a 5 and 10 lira store and really had fun looking around in it. Finally left Florence at 1630 and arrived back here at 1800. Around 2100 my jaw started aching and by bedtime I had a heck of a toothache.

Thursday, January 18

Caught the ambulance to the hospital to get my tooth looked at. That ride seemed twice as long because my tooth was killing me. After looking it over, the dentist said it was completely rotten and had to come out. He gave me some shots which deadened my jaw and then took the tooth out. It was as simple as that. Went to chow at 1730 and took over some clothes and shoes I had collected from the boys for the Italians working in our mess hall.

Friday, January 19

Doc Lowenstein, our Group Doctor, told me a few things that he wanted done about disinfecting the dishes and glasses in the Mess Hall and bar.

At 1700 I washed up, shaved and got all dressed up for the dance tonight. At 2000 I checked to see if everything was all set for the party. Everything was O.K., but the band was late. By 2115 we were really sweating them out when they walked in. Our party was another small one, but the best part was when two of the pilots sat in with the band and had a terrific jam session.

Saturday, January 20

Looked over the map showing the progress of the war. I hope the Russians can keep up their drive and, Maybe the war will be over soon. We have to bomb a railroad in the Brenner Pass today. We took off at 1235 and got to our target an hour later. Brenner Pass is notoriously famous for its flak, but we didn't get any at all. It is also the gateway out of northern Italy and an important route for the Germans.

Today was a big day up there. There were 34 B-25s bombing and about 60 P-47s dive bombing this afternoon. On the way back, we escorted some of the B-25s. We also found a German car on the road which exploded after we strafed it.. As we flew past, a few Italians waved at us.

Landed and was interrogated and was told that my promotion had come through. I was now a First Lieutenant. Judy will be tickled when she hears about it. Got to the Club and bought two bar cards and told Joe, the bartender to give all my friends drinks as they came in and take it off my card.

Sunday, January 21

I'm flying "Little Puss", my plane, for the first time in a long while. She really was purring sweetly. We got over the Po River when my wingman started having trouble with his prop so I had to take him home. We did some strafing and level bombing of a road on the way. We didn't miss it by much.

Went to supper at 1730 and made plans with the Mess Sergeant for a birthday party tomorrow night for all the men whose birthdays are in this month.

Monday, January 22

I wasn't scheduled to fly today, but at 1400 they needed someone to test hop an airplane, so I took off at 1500 and wrung the plane out and landed at 1530. Got my notice of another cluster to my Air Medal when I got back.

By 1800 everyone was ready to sit down, so I read off the names of the men who had birthdays this month and we all sang "Happy Birthday" for them. The party was a big success, and everyone liked the idea. This was something I decided to do each month after I became Mess Officer.

Tuesday, January 23

On the early mission. Briefed and took off at 0755. Our target is a warehouse in the middle of the PO Valley in the town of Ostiglia which is supposed to be a hot spot. We came over the target and dived. Most of our bombs hit the warehouse, but some hit the town.

When we pulled off, I still had one bomb that hadn't come off and so did one of the other boys, so on the way home, we bombed a railroad yard at Corfu. My bomb hit right on the tracks, but the other fellow's wouldn't come off. When we got home, I took him out to sea and he tried to drop it there, but it still wouldn't come off. We finally came back and all landed and he had to circle till everyone was in and then he landed safely.

After supper, we had a dry run for the presentation of another unit citation which takes place tomorrow.

Wednesday, January 24

After breakfast, I supervised getting the place ready for the General's visit today. At 1000 everything was all set, and it looked really nice. At 1030, I got a phone call from headquarters saying the whole works was called off until tomorrow, so we had to rearrange the whole Mess Hall again. Because of the General's visit today, I had the main meal served at noon and everyone like the idea. Got letters from everyone back home telling about the Christmas and birthday party at Judy's house. Wish I could have been there.

Thursday, January 25

Checked to see if everything was set up for the General's visit. At 1115 we got word that the damn General wasn't coming again. Later one of the Italian speaking G.I.s in the Mess Hall took me to a place in town where I picked up a couch. After supper, I made arrangements with him to get more furniture for our room.

Friday, January 26

Nothing was doing today because of the bad weather again. Mike, the Italian speaking G.I. took me to a furniture place where we got two leather easy chairs, a desk and a double decker bed. After supper I dressed for the party. We had a great band and the party was a good one.

Saturday, January 27

We all went down to the line to be briefed for the first mission of the day. Our target today was a rail bridge at Cismon in the Alps.

We took off at 0745 and bombed our target with no enemy action to worry about. Then recce the Po Valley on the way back and were able to shoot up some tank cars and then came home. Landed at 1000 and was interrogated. Nothing much doing for the rest of the day.

Sunday, January 28

The weather cleared up beautifully, but we were stood down because our runway is being resurfaced. At 1100 we had a pilots meeting and we were shown the new camera that is going to be installed in our plane. If it's as good as they say, we should get some excellent pictures.

After lunch, Reece, Reasman and I set out to climb a nearby mountain. We really picked a job for ourselves. We crossed the Orno River in a very ingenious ferry for five lira and then proceeded to climb. It took us an hour and 15 minutes to get to an old cabin on top. I was sweating and my feet felt like lead. It was worth it though because the view was superb. After a little target practice, we headed back home.

Monday, January 29

We got a hurry call just as we arrived at the line and we took off at 0720 before the sun came up. About 250 Motor Transport were reported moving north all night out of Milan. We were told to rush up there to see what we could find and radio back the results. We didn't find anything in the PO Valley, so we recce all the roads leading into the Alps.

We found about six German tanks and 15 trucks parked on one road, so we dive bombed them with good results. Instead of pulling up, we stayed at 4,000 feet and went south in the Lake Como Valley.

The mountains were on both sides of us and the valley was only one mile wide, so we couldn't do too much maneuvering. On the way back, we saw what looked like trucks lined up under some trees, so the flight leader made a pass on them and I took my element down on them. No results were observed. When we got out into the PO Valley, we saw a string of boxcars. We were all set to go down on them when we saw four other P-47s down there, so we left them alone.

We were getting ready to go home when we saw this locomotive with eight passenger cars heading north, so we swung around to get it. It went into a long train shed and came out the other end going hell bent for election. The flight leader and his wing man finished off the locomotive on the first pass so I took my wingman down on the cars. We came down for a second pass and saw troops pouring out of the cars. The locomotive had blown up by this time and we concentrated on making German sausage out of those soldiers. We left beaucoup of them in a shitpile. We had to go home then because my wingman was very low on gas.

We had General Darcy to supper tonight, so we started the movie at 1915 so that he could see the gun camera films.

Tuesday, January 30

Gave instructions for getting the Club fixed up for the General's visit. At 1120 he arrived and everyone came to attention. The ceremony was simple. Our citation was read off and then General Cannon tied a streamer to our group flag, and that's all there was to it. After the ceremony everyone had lunch. Then the General's party began leaving.

The colonel introduced me to the General and told him that I was in charge of the Club. We shook hands and he told me that he liked the Club very much. After dinner we spent the evening with some South African pilots at their Club. It turned out to be one of the best evenings in a long time.

Wednesday, January 31

I saw that I wasn't scheduled, so I went to the lounge and had some doughnuts and coffee. Then I was interviewed for a story to be sent to my hometown newspapers. Luke, the P.R. officer says he is planning a big story about me because of my two jobs, but he will not tell me what it's about. After lunch I spent about an hour going over the books with Dusty who is my clerk in the Club. We have to get them ready for the inspectors who are coming up from the 12th Air Force to inspect us.

Chapter 8 – February 1945

Thursday, February 1

Went down to the line at 0900, but nothing was doing because of the bad weather again. Finally got a jeep and went to the PX to buy my PX rations and then came home. Went to the Mess Hall and spent the lunch hour collecting bar and mess bills. Had a pilots meeting. For a change we had a good meeting discussing the rockets we are beginning to use. Went to the Mess Hall at 1730 and spent the supper hour collecting bills. Ate supper and saw the most recent gun camera films.

Friday, February 2

The weather is lousy again, so they didn't bother waking us for the early mission. I went up to the orderly room and sent home the plaque that I had made. Also sent $100 to dad and changed my allotment so that $275 a month goes to Judy. Heard we were stood down for the rest of the day. The party wasn't bad this week. They seem to be improving every time. A bunch of the South Africans came up also. Most of them are pretty nice fellows.

Saturday, February 3

It's so foggy this morning that we could hardly see 100 feet in front of us. At 1030 Luke brought in the photographer who was going to take pictures of our club. Got all of the Italian waiters together and through an interpreter I laid down the law to them about their work and actions around the Club. After lunch, I spoke to Major Cameron about one of our cooks who I want to get rid of because his drunkenness and missing shifts. Major Cameron is going to talk to him.

The inspectors came this afternoon and checked all our books and liquor supply, and aside from a few minor mistakes everything was in good order.

Sunday, February 4

Took off at 1010 to bomb a small rail bridge on the main line out of Trento. The bridge is only three and a half miles from the town and right on the Brenner Line, so we all expected to catch some flak. Made it up there O.K. and bombed without any results and then came home. No flak. I haven't flown in about five days now and didn't feel very much at ease today.

Had supper and just as I finished one of the cooks came for me. I knew that something was up, because he was very excited. He said that some outfit near here had one of our cooks and they were beating him up .I rushed upstairs and got a carbine and a couple of clips of ammo from one of the cooks.

Captain Casselman took another carbine and we set out for the outfit. On the way there, we met our cook coming back escorted by a crowd of Italians. We all went to the Club and Major Cameron gave our cook a good bawling out for not minding his own business. It seems that he was trying to rescue an Italian boy who was being held because they say he had stolen some gas. Thank goodness it did not develop into a bad situation.

Monday, February 5

I was on the second mission. The weather was so bad that the first mission hadn't taken off. We spent the morning sitting around. I didn't feel well this morning. I felt strange and nauseas and it seems that most of the officers felt the same way. It must have been something in our food, so I asked Doc to check up on it. We were briefed at 1300. We went out to our ships and were just getting ready to go when our first flight came back with its bombs, so our mission was called back.

Tuesday, February 6

We took off at1300 for another mission to the Brenner Pass and after climbing through some scattered clouds over the field, we headed out on course. As we were taking off a report came over the radio about enemy planes at the Brenner Pass. That's where we were going.

We really kept our eyes open, but we didn't see a darned thing. Bombed with good results and then came home. We had to circle our field for 40 minutes before we could come in and land because there was so much air traffic. One of our squadrons caught 50 ME 109s in the Po Valley and shot down three of them and got one probable.

Wednesday, February 7

Today was a beautiful Spring day and nearly everyone is flying. I hung around OPs for awhile and then wrote some letters home. After lunch, I read for awhile and went back to the line. I was on a mission to hit a rail diversion on the Brenner Line which we have been hitting for the past few days. Everything went along smoothly and the mission, my 61st, was a milk run. When we came in to land, I was too close to the second man, so I went around. The tower told me to stay up till they called me, so for about 20 minutes I buzzed our Mess Hall and all the surrounding towns.

Went down to the line and saw that I was on the 1225 mission, so I hung around. At 1000 I went to the Pilots Lounge and had some coffee and doughnuts, and then Luke, our Public Relations Officer came and got me. It seems that General Cannon was coming here today and we were going to have a big ceremony for the 500,000 sortie to be flown by the Mediterranean Air Force. I am going to be the one to fly the 500,000 sortie. This is the big deal that Luke had in store for me.

I dashed back to my room and shaved. At 1100, I went to eat. After eating, I went back down to the line and met all the officers who are the General's photographers. We briefed on the show we were going to put on when we landed, and then we were briefed on our mission. It was a Rover Joe in support of a push in the Senclo Valley.

We took off at 1225 and called Rover Joe. He gave us some tanks to look for in a nearby valley, but after spending about 15 minutes looking for them, we gave up and called for another target. He gave us some gun positions on a point of land on the coast to bomb with our fire bombs. We had to glide bomb, so we came down from about 5,000 feet till we were about 100 feet off the water, and then we headed in. The whole hillside seemed to be full of light ack-ack all shooting at us. Lieutenant Young was in front of me, and just as he let his bombs go, he was hit in the left wing and the door to his ammunition boxes blew off. He started what looked like a climbing turn to the left. Then he slow rolled right into the hillside and his plane exploded. He probably killed lots of Germans and he got a few guns, but that's doing it the hard way.

We came off the target and called Rover Joe and told him we were going home. When we got back, we had to circle for about 20 minutes before they finally let us come in. We held perfect formation and we came in about ten feet above the runway. Our peel-up was a beauty and they got good movies of it.

When we landed, we parked at the end of the runway where the General was waiting for us. We got out of the planes and General Cannon shook hands with us. Then we all walked over to the microphone. The movie cameras were grinding away all the time. We talked in front of the mike for awhile, and the General told me that I had flown the half millionth sortie for the Mediterranean Tactical Air Forces.

After we were finished taking movies, they started taking still pictures of the General, Colonel Nevitt, some English colonel and me. When we finished those, the photographers took pictures of me in front of my plane with my crew chief, who had painted ½ million on the side of the plane, and some of me alone. All in all they spent about an hour taking pictures. I think I'm the most photographed man on the field now.

When it was finally over, I went back to the OPs and signed a statement about how Lieutenant Young went in. The ack-ack boys gave us a scare this evening. They were shooting their guns for about an hour. It was a beautiful light show of fireworks, but got us all pretty nervous.

Friday, February 9

Nothing much doing down the line so I went to the Lounge and had some coffee and doughnuts. Went down to the photo lab and saw some of the pictures that were taken yesterday.

Later I went to a pilots meeting at which we had an interesting talk on artillery spotting from a sub. Interesting but had no bearing on anything we do. At night I went to the party. For a change, we had good food and a swell five piece band. The dance floor was crowded all night.

Saturday, February 10

Our mission today was to escort some bombers. We were all tickled about it, because it's a good chance to run into enemy fighters, but the mission was suddenly called off. We were briefed for another mission and took off at 1330 but couldn't get to our target because of weather. We bombed a bridge near La Spezia harbor and caught some flak, but no one got hurt.

I had to be at a meeting where we were alerted and told that we will move in about 48 hours. I found out that we are going back to "La Belle France" to support a big push there.

Sunday, February 11

Made up a list of men from the Mess Hall who were to go on the advance party and submitted it to the colonel and then came back and got the boys started on packing. At 1230 they told me that we wouldn't leave till Wednesday, so we held off on packing. Spent most of the afternoon showing the furniture to one of the Red Cross girls who is going to buy it. Finally completed all arrangements for selling the furniture and giving back everything we borrowed from the local Italians.

Monday, February 12

Was awakened at 0530 for a mission, but the weather was so lousy we didn't do much of anything. Had lunch and then showed our bar to a captain from some quartermaster outfit who wants to buy it. Went to the Service Group Finance Office and paid off all our bills for the Mess. Captain Weikert, the Mess Officer, came back from the hospital today, so we had a talk after supper. Got a letter from home today giving Morty's A.P.O. number. I hope he comes over here so that I can get to see him.

Tuesday, February 13

Drew a week's rations for the boys who are going on the advance party with me. I got called to the telephone and was surprised when I found Sheldon Mayer on the phone. He's one of the old Aqueduct gang from the Bronx. He's in the 350th Fighter Group down in Pisa and he's working in Special Services. He came up here after the call and we had a nice talk about old times. I took him to lunch at our Mess and then he left. One of our boys got jumped by a bunch of G.I.s today, so I got a gun and eight of us went over there. By then, things had quieted down, so we didn't do anything. Our boy had a black eye, but he was O.K.

La Belle France -*From February 14 until February 23, we were moving from Italy to our new base in France.*

Wednesday, February 14

Today is Judy and my second wedding anniversary and look where I am. I miss my sweetie.

Our truck has to pull Major Cameron's trailer, so I got the key from him just in case things got rough, so I'd have a place to stay. By 1230, we were lined up on the docks at Leghorn and found out we had a long wait.

By 1500 we drove our truck and trailer on board and then onto an elevator which took us up to the top deck. After about half an hour of maneuvering, we finally got crammed into position. I wonder how we will get it out now.

Thursday February 15

We made plans for debarking and then turned in all our Italian money so that it could be changed. I found out about one of my cooks screwing off roll call last night and put him on K.P. till we land.

We are on an LST-211, U.S. Navy. These navy officers really live right. They have a Mess Room that seats 18 officers very comfortably with beautiful dishes, silverware and very good service. After dinner we had a meeting and were told a few rules we would have to observe while we were on board.

Friday, February 16

The French coast was in sight. At 1100 we started unloading, and by 1230 the whole works were off the boat and assembled in a big lot about three blocks from the dock. We really worked fast getting our vehicles off the boat, because we were all hoping to have extra time to spend in Marseilles. It was no go though because by 1300 we were off to a staging area. After an hours drive we got to our staging area which is about 15 miles north of Marseilles. I went to headquarters at the staging area and found out that our group had top priority, so I didn't have any trouble getting a truck and drew a ten day supply of food rations for the group and 625 gallons of gas. I got a big kick out of drawing those tremendous quantities of food and gas. Found we didn't have enough gas, so I had to go down again and get another 200 gallons.

We are pulling Major Cameron's trailer, so I'm using it to sleep in. This staging area is a tremendous place and is being built by German P.W.s. It's going to be the biggest staging area in this theater. When we pulled in, everyone got right to work and by the time I was back with the food and gas, our cooks had everything unpacked and a meal was almost ready.

Saturday, February 17

I rode in the colonel's car which is a 1937 Ford and believe me it was comfortable and fairly warm. It was pretty foggy and dark when we started out and the convoy was pretty well scattered out all over the countryside. One incident was a classic. We came to one fork in the road and found one officer in a jeep parked there. We asked him which way the convoy went and he in a very helpless voice said. "They went both ways." He looked as if he was ready to cry. By 0930 we had gotten on the main road and the convoy was reformed. At 1130 we caught up with our kitchen trucks which had gone ahead, and they prepared lunch alongside the road. My boys from the Club as soon as the convoy stopped went to the nearby farmhouse and bought some fresh eggs, and instead of army rations, we filled a can with gas and cooked ourselves three eggs and bacon a piece. We are 40 miles south of Lyon, and I had a chance to go to Lyon tonight, but I passed it up because it would have been and long cold ride. The reason we are back in France is because General Patton asked for the 27th Fighter Group to support his tanks. I guess we have a good reputation. There are rumors that we're going to support a big push on the 23rd of February. I hope the rumor s true.

Sunday, February 18

At 0900 we were passing through Lyon and everyone was praying that something would happen to stop us there for awhile. No such luck though. We rode all morning and stopped for a brief lunch. While we were eating, crowds of French kids gathered around. We couldn't help but give them candy and food which they loved.

At 1715 we pulled into the bivouac area at Dijon and found it a sea of mud. We tried to get permission to continue on our way, but it was no go. One of our officers got to talking with a French girl, and she invited us to her house for supper. Five of us took a bunch of food and went there. Those people do wonders with this army chow of ours. They also brought out beaucoup white and red wines, pickles and cakes. Everything was marvelous. When we tried to offer them something for their trouble, they nearly became insulted. Their answer was, "We are so happy you are here, we can't do enough for you."

Monday, February 19

We drove all morning through some of the prettiest country I've seen in a long time. It is the area between Dijon and Chalon. After lunch, three others and I took off in the Colonel's car to beat the convoy to our new field. We arrived there at 1400 to find we were the first to pull in there. The new field is at St. Dizier and it is tremendous. There is one other outfit on the field and they fly P-38s but are changing over to P-47s. We found that the service group had expected us to arrive with no equipment, so they had put up tents, mess hall, a supply dump, lights and just about everything for us.

The only part that we don't have are Officers Billets because the other outfits have requisitioned everything in town. We do have a place for a Mess and Club that is just like a juke joint back home. It's a hotel in town, and our Mess is going to be in its restaurant and our club in its bar. I moved into the hotel temporarily, because for the next two days I have to get it ready for use.

Tuesday, February 20

Picked up my boys. Brought our stuff into town and started them unloading trucks. Then hunted around and found rooms for them in a small hotel near our mess. Had a long talk with the owner of our hotel and started him getting our place set up. After lunch, I took the cooks over to their hotel and got them set up there. Then I sent the manager of our place out to round up civilian workers for our mess. By 1830 all was finished and I was really tired.

Wednesday, February 21

None of our transports or planes have arrived yet. Our planes aren't due for an hour yet, so I went back to town and told the boys to get supper cooking. At 1600 our planes and transports started coming in. Found the transport with our mess equipment and got it all loaded on a truck and rushed to the mess hall where we were ready to serve at 1900. The dinner was good, but our waitresses need some education and have to be shown what to do.

Thursday, February 22

A meeting of all our pilots was all about our radio procedure around here and then a short lecture on escape. At 1930 we had another meeting on escape which is important now that we will be flying over Germany.

The lecture lasted till 2100. It was the most interesting and entertaining lecture we had in a long time. The speaker was from Secret Service who had been in and out of Germany several times. Before the war, he had been a magician, so after his lecture, he did some card tricks to entertain us.

Friday, February 23

I'm scheduled on the second mission today, but we only hung around for awhile because the weather was bad and everything was called off.

Saturday, February 24

Found out this morning that the Mess Officer is being transferred to another department, so I am in complete charge, and I'm to pick my own assistant. After lunch they called me to come down to the line, because the weather is clearing.

Finally, at 1630 we took off on a mission We were to recce some rail lines East of the Rhine River, but when we neared our target, it was covered over, so the controller told us to jettison our bombs and try to make it home before dark. We really went all out and got back just as darkness was closing in.

Sunday, February 25

Got a lift down to the line at 1000 and hung around talking about tactics until 1130 when we were briefed for a mission. We finally took off at 1415. We circled the field once and then tucked it in real tight and climbed through the clouds. We headed out on course, and as we got near the Rhine, two of the boys had to turn back because of engine trouble, so that left 14 of us. After we crossed the bomb line, we spotted a train in a station. Eight of us dive bombed it and then made one strafing run. We left it very well clobbered. After we formed up, someone yelled something about "beaucoup bogies" and when I looked back I saw two MEs pulling up into the clouds. They had hit two of our boys, so they left us and went home. The remaining ships dive bombed and strafed some trucks, and then we all went home. When we landed, we found that Reece had been slightly wounded in the arm.

Monday, February 26

Started to take off at 0830, but half way down the runway we were called back because of lousy weather. The ceiling keeps lowering and the clouds just keep closing in. We were told to stand by. At 1030 we had a pilots meeting and talked about radio procedure and all missions were called off.

Tuesday, February 27

At 1600 two men from the Counter Intelligence control came to see me about one of our waitresses. It seems that she had been an interpreter for the Germans, and since they left, she has been closely watched. They feel that she still may be in contact with them, but they can't get enough evidence to throw her into jail, so they are having her watched. They told me to get rid of her. After they left, I told Mr. Boidet, the proprietor to fire her and get another girl to replace her. That was our excitement for the day.

Wednesday, February 28

We went down to the line where I got my parachute refitted. Then went to the Mess hall and started making arrangement for the birthday party for the boys whose birthdays fall in February.

We briefed and took off at 1430. This is the first mission for my new plane and it flies beautifully. We got up over the bomb line and were halfway through our recce when we spotted some MEs diving on us. We broke into them and formed a big buffberry. They couldn't get at us, and we tried to climb up to them but couldn't get there fast enough. We had dropped our bombs and belly tanks so that we would be more maneuverable. When they saw that they took off and as soon as they left, we formed up and went home.

Chapter 9 – March 1945

Thursday, March 1

Was awakened at 6:45 in time to eat and get to the line to be briefed for a mission. Took off around 8:30 but we could not get to our target because of clouds so we called the controller for an "egg basket". That is blind bombing directed by the controller. Following his instructions we finally dropped our bombs and headed home. After we landed I was told to hurry to the Operations tent because I was scheduled on another mission. We were briefed and went to our planes and we were told to stand by. Hung around till 11:30 and then were told to eat lunch and be back for a 12;30 briefing.

Took off at 13:40 and our mission was to go to an area around Mannheim to provide cover for about 500 bombers that were bombing the city. We stayed there for about 45 minutes while a steady stream of bombers pasted the city and because no enemy fighters showed up we had nothing to do so we headed home. When we got back to the field it was raining very hard and there was low cloud cover so we had to circle for awhile before we finally got to land. Finally landed, were interrogated and then headed to the mess hall for supper.

After supper had another conference with Mr. Baidet and raised a little hell about the way I wanted things done. Spent some time giving out PX Rations and at 20:00 Major Chairs called me up to his room.

He told me that he had heard from C.I.C. that we had another girl working here who had been a collaborationist and we had to fire her. We had a nice talk after that and I finally got down and closed the PX at 21:30.

Had a glass of beer and then back to my tent and hit the sack.

Friday, March 2

Woke at 7:30 but it was so cold I stayed in the sack till 8:45, got up and had 2 Hershey bars for breakfast and then went down to catch the bus to the field. Briefed for a mission at 10:30 and while we were getting ready to go to our planes a plane came in with only one wheel down and the pilot did a beautiful job of crash landing it with no damage to the runway.

We took off at 11:30 and flew up to Nancy to meet the B26's that we were escorting to their bomb run. Went into Germany with them and after they bombed the target we headed back to France. We saw two German ME's under the bomber formation but they made no move to attack so we continued our escort job. Landed and was briefed and had lunch. After lunch sat around for awhile shooting the bull and finally went to the office and gave out some PX rations. After that the Mess Sgt. and I checked all the stuff that we have and made a list of stuff that was missing.

At 17:00 came back, washed up had supper and then had a talk with the hotel manager to straighten a few things and the Dusty and I got the books up to date. Finished at 21:00 came back and wrote a few letters and then hit to sack.

Saturday, March 3

Awoke at 7:30 to freezing cold. Dressed, shivered, went to breakfast and then down to the line to be briefed for a mission. On my way out to the plane I stopped at Tech Supply and drew a pair on sunglasses. Took off at 9:15 on an escort mission. Met 55 B26's at 9:50 to escort them to Germany, but because of heavy cloud cover they were unable to find their target so we escorted them back to friendly territory and we headed home and landed. Were interrogated, had lunch and went to the club office and had a long bull session with Lt. Gannon who is chairman of the club committee.

At 15:00 came back upstairs and the two girls that were fired were waiting for me. They were the collaborationists and they wanted to know why they had been fired. I told them it was the Colonels orders and shooed them out. Went over to see the Sgt. In charge of the Ration dump. Gave him a bottle of whiskey in return for all the good rations he is going to give us from now on. Had supper at 18:00 and then gave out PX rations to fellows who had not received theirs. Got my pay...$159 for the month. Went up to Doc L's room and shaved and went back to the tent where we made some soup and had a few rolls and jam. Hit the sack at 23:15.

Sunday, March 4

Was awakened at 5:45 for a mission. Got up and lit the stove because it was cold as the devil. Dressed, had breakfast and went to the line to be briefed for a mission and then we had to stand by because of bad weather. We all went into the Pilot tent, lit the stove and lay back in the beach chairs we have there and listened to the radio. Pretty soon most of us had dozed off.

Got up around 9:00 and we decided to go to the Group Dispensary to get the the radium treatment they were offering to prevent colds. After the treatment I went to Group Operations to arrange for a B25 to go to the town of Cognac tomorrow to buy liquor for the club. Went back to the line and then to lunch. Had lunch, wrote a long letter to Judy and then went to Group Ops. and found out the we can take the B25 tomorrow if the weather is OK.

Had supper and then phoned the squadron to get one of our boys who speaks French very well to take him as an interpreter tomorrow. Came back to the tent and wrote a letter home and hit the sack at 23:00.

Monday, March 5

Awoke at 7:30 but couldn't get out of bed till 8:00 because it was so cold. Went to mess hall, had breakfast and then back to pack my musette bag with the necessary travel items for the next few days. Went to the flight line but the weather is so bad our trip to Cognac to buy liquor for the officers club had to be cancelled. Checked for mail at Operations and found 35 letters for me, mostly from Judy.

One of them had a color picture of Judy in her new fur coat and she looks great. I was like a proud papa showing them around. Called the mess hall and asked one of the boys to bring the truck to pick me up because I had gotten a wooden door for our tent and a bucket seat from a damaged plane that we were going to make an easy chair out of.

After lunch Dusty and I picked up the officers liquor ration and prepared it for distribution. Each officer is entitled to 2 bottles of Scotch, I bottle of Champagne and I bottle of Gin and some of the guys had nerve enough to bitch because there was no whiskey. The entire ration only costs them $8.00.

Read most of my letters while giving out the ration and then stored the remaining stock in the storeroom and closed up for the night. I caught a cold and it has really knocked me out.   Hit the sack at 23:00.

Tuesday, March 6

Awoke at 7:30 by Reasman coming into the tent. He had been up for an early mission but they were told to stand by in quarters because of bad weather. Around 11:00 we finally made our plans for the day. Reasman took the burner from the stove down to the line to try and get one of the mechanics to fix it for us. Got Frederick, the new boy in the tent to work on building a door for the tent. My cold still has me knocked out.

Spent the rest of the afternoon writing long letters to Judy and the folks answering all their mail. After supper the Mess Sgt. Told me about a fight two of the men had in the kitchen. I called the one who had been at fault and took his pass for the night away from him. Later he came back to me shaking like a leaf. I took him up to Doc who gave him a sedative and sent him back to go to sleep. Doc told me that he was mentally unstable and we would have to watch him. Back to the tent, had some soup and crackers, and welcomed Reece who came back from the hospital today.

Wednesday, March 7

Woke around 8:30 dressed, had some breakfast and went to the Mess Hall for coffee. Went up to Doc L room to shave and wash up. Had a talk with the fellow who had caused all the trouble last night and he was still a nervous wreck so I sent him to see Doc again. He came back later to tell me that Doc was sending him to the hospital for observation. After he left I picked up my laundry and then to the Mess for lunch. After lunch Col. Nevitt came into the dining room. He was in a very talkative mood so we shot the bull for awhile.

Went down to the office and typed a list of the stuff we lost on the last move and then sent Dusty down to

149

headquarters with it. I saw the Sgt. From the ration dump and gave him a bottle of cognac in return for extra rations for the Saturday night party. After supper just hung around the bar chewing the fat and speculating with the guys about the rumors of our coming move.

Thursday, March 8

Was awakened at 7:15 by one of our guys who was going up to the front as an Air Support Officer. Had breakfast and then I gave him extra cigarettes and candy to take with him to trade with. After breakfast the Mess Sgt. told me we had a lot of sugar and jam missing so we decided to examine the bags of our waitresses and we found it all. They come to work each day with empty bags and try to take home full ones. They are so dumb but I gathered them together, bawled them all out and threatened to fire anyone caught stealing.

Borrowed a typewriter and paper and spent several hours answering the accumulation of mail that I had received. Reece and I had saved a bottle of champagne which we decided to drink with supper and it made us both feel very good. I had to go to a meeting for an hour to discuss our coming move and plan the shipment of our mess material. Hit the sack around 23:00.

Friday, March 9

Woke around 9:00 and Reece and I had a cup of coffee on the way to a meeting called for at the flight line at 10:00. The weather is lousy again today but an early mission managed to get off. The meeting was called off till tonight. We are all wondering what is about.

Stopped at the Labor Bureau to try to find out why our civilian employees had not been paid. Someone had screwed up and the proper papers had not been submitted so I had to go to Chalon to see the area Eng. Office about it. Had lunch first and had Mr. Boidet get me the records for our employees. Borrowed Maj. Chairs jeep and Dusty, Reece and I took off for Chalon, about 50 miles away. Arrived there and saw Maj. Duncan and was able to get everything straightened out. It really was very simple but we had to wait about an hour while they were typing out the papers needed to take care of the problem.

We rode around town for awhile which was very nice and we decided to see if we could find some cognac to buy but there was none to be found. Had a snack at the transient mess and then went to pick up the papers. They weren't ready so I made arrangements for them to be sent to me tomorrow and we went back to our base. Had a talk with Maj. Chairs and got permission to go to Paris tomorrow to see if I could buy some cognac. Called the motor pool and made arrangements for a jeep and back to the sack around 23:00

Saturday, March 10

Up at 5:45 dressed and took a jeep parked at the next tent down to the field to pick up my jeep for the trip to Paris. Came back, had breakfast, had the jeep washed by the boys who work in the kitchen and Mike (our bartender) and I took off for Paris.

Pulled into Paris around 10:00. Paris is magnificent in that it is so much like New York. First thing we did was get a requisition for gas and get the jeep filled again. Then we started looking around for a place to buy cognac. Found a store that had some so we bought 64 bottles at $10 per bottle. Afterwards I sold them 4 cartons of cigarettes and 2 boxes of chocolates for $80 to get some of our money back.

Mike happened to say something in Italian and the next I knew he and the storekeeper were jabbering away like long lost friends. We were invited to dinner at his friends nite club, which was a charming little place. His friend turned out to be a charming woman, about 25 years old, and a wonderful hostess. It was a leisurely meal and we all talked quite a bit and my French is improving. After dinner, the woman whose name was Elaine, took us to her friends shop, a perfumerie. On the way we passed a florist and we bought her a bunch of flowers. There wasn't anything at her friends store so we said our goodbyes and at 16:30 we left wonderful Paris.

Got back to our base by 20:00 because the darn jeep kept stalling. Made it just in time to get cleaned up for the squadron party that had been planned. Got a little drunk and Reasman and I put on a jitterbug session for everyone. At 2:00 the bar was closed and I was sober enough to make sure the club was closed. Hit the sack at 3:15.

Sunday, March 11

Slept late and then went to the Mess Hall for lunch. Met Reasman and spent some time playing gin rummy. Finally went to the storage area and prepared lots of empty bottles to take with me to Cognac tomorrow.

Our squadron move has been temporarily called off so I going to make the trip to Cognac as planned. Phoned Operations and made all the necessary arrangements for the trip tomorrow. One of our waitresses came in and was telling us about the day our planes bombed this airfield when the Germans were here, and she told us how the French people came out to cheer us on, much to the Germans chagrin.

Very quiet all day and after supper supervised the ration issue to men returning from rest camp. Brought this diary up to date and hit the sack.

Monday, March 12

Up early and Reece and I went to breakfast and then gathered my overnite stuff for the trip to Cognac. Went down to the line and got our orders typed and then drew $2500 of the Club money from the safe. Went to the B25 that we were going to use and loaded the empty cognac bottles and our overnite bags into the plane. The crew chiefs weren't there yet so we went back to the mess hall for a quick snack and were back to the plane before noon and took off.

After we were airborne I took over as co-pilot all the way to Cognac. Landed at 13:30 in a meadow near the distillery and were met by a French official and the first words out of his mouth were "Have you eaten yet?" He then took us to the Commandants office where they provided us with a car and a chauffer. Our first stop was the Hennessey distillery where we arranged for 5 cases of Cognac and when we came out our car had a flat tire which took nearly an hour to get fixed. We then went to another famous distillery, Martell and made arrangements to return tomorrow with all our empty bottles.

Went back to the field and picked up our enlisted men from the crew and went to the commandants office. I brought him 5 packs of cigarettes and he was delighted. He had made arrangements for 7 of us to spend the night at Mr. Martell's mansion. Drove out there at 18:30 and the place is magnificent. A millionaires home and Reece and I are sharing the most beautiful room imaginable. There must be over 40 rooms in this mansion and it is truly a palace.

There are thick rugs everywhere and the drapes are very beautiful. After getting our rooms set we went back to the field and had a good French meal with plenty of wine and then back to the house at 21:00. Mr. Martell was waiting for us and invited us to have a drink with him and his wife. They had both been to America and spoke English very well. He was very friendly, told us many jokes and finally said good night at 22:30. I did not realize at the time what a famous person he was. Bon Soir!

Tuesday, March 13

Awakened at 8:15 by Lt. Gannon. Washed and dressed and Reece and I rode out to the field with a Major who was with another group that had also come to buy Cognac. We finagled a truck from the French army by bribing with 2 cartons of cigarettes. Went to the Martell distillery and finally got 5 more cases of cognac. By using cigarettes for favors we got things done pretty fast.

At noon we went back to the field where they had a French transient mess hall set up and we had a great meal. The French are very leisurely in everything they do, especially eating. One of the boys said "the French don't win wars but they sure are a happy bunch" Went back to the distillery and picked up the cognac to take to the plane. By then it was too late to take off so we had a light supper and then a bunch of is piled into the jeep and went to the Martell mansion. Went back and picked up the rest of our guys and settled in for the night. Got a pitcher of hot water and shaved and washed up. Mr. Martell's son came in and gave us beautiful pictures of the house as souvenirs of our visit. To sleep at 2300.

Wednesday, March 14

Up early and had to wait for transportation to the field. Made arrangements for another truck and went back to town for a final try to buy more cognac. Finally bought 3 more cases at black market prices but we now had plenty and went back and got ready to take off. Finally took off at 13:30 and buzzed the town, the field and Mr. Martell's house and then headed on a course north to get back to our base.

We did OK till we came to the Rhone river and we turned north when we should have turned south. Our gas was getting low when we finally spotted an air strip to land at. We found out that we were 100 miles north of the LeBron Airfield at Lyon. After a brief conference we decided to try to make it to Lyon before searching for gas. That was a half hour of sweating I do not want to have to do again. We finally spotted LeBron and had only 50 gallons of gas left for both engines. There were beaucoup B-26's going in to land, but could not wait so we cut into the traffic pattern and landed with our gas gauged showing only 25 gallons. Got our plane serviced and gassed up and sent an R O N (remain over night) back to our home field.

Got our stuff together, locked up the plane and took the bus into Lyon. We dropped Reece off at his girlfriend's house and we went to the Billeting office and got rooms at the Grand Nouvel Hotel which was a beauty. Washed up and then Gannon and I took a walk around Lyon, stopped at a café, had a beer and then returned to meet the rest of our crew and had supper.

At supper we met an American civilian Named Frank Warren who works for O.S.S.(Office of Strategic Services). He is one of the boys who have been working behind the lines in France for the past year.

He really had some interesting stories to tell and we let him do most of the talking. He said that if people knew about some of the things that they did behind the lines, they would not get so excited about German atrocities. We went to several bars and had champagne at each one, $35 worth. Finally ended the night at 1:00.

Thursday, March 15

Awakened by hotel telephone and at breakfast met another pilot and threw the bull with him for awhile. Went down to the barber shop and had the luxury of a haircut, shampoo, shave and massage. Got our stuff together and we caught a bus to the field. Checked the weather and then went out to the plane. Had some K rations and then pre-flighted the plane. Everything was OK so we took off at 11:45 and flew the "iron beam" (rail lines) back to our base.

Landed at 13:00 and called Ops for a jeep to get to the mess hall for lunch. Then took a truck to unload the plane and took it back and unloaded at the Mess Hall. Everyone is flying today because of the big push that has started. I start flying missions again tomorrow. We had left the truck outside the Mess Hall and when we went out it was gone. Hope I don't get into trouble for it.

After supper we had mail call and I got "beaucoup" mail. Morty is here in France in the Infantry and I can't wait to get his A.P.O. so that I can get to see him. Came back to the tent and read mail and hit the sack.

Friday, March 16

Up early and went to the Mess Hall, had breakfast and spoke to the Mess Sgt. about what he had to do to get ready for our coming move. Went down to the flight line and was briefed for a mission. Had to wait for the early mission to land and the planes to be serviced before we could take off. We are operating at full capacity today because of the 7th Army push into Germany. Out to our planes at 10:30 and watched the crew chiefs finish their service and finally took off at 11:15. We were on a search mission to look for targets of opportunity. Finally found a rail yard that had some train movement, dove on it dropped our bombs and scored two direct hits. Flak from the Germans was scant and inaccurate. After bombing the train yard we stayed low and strafed through the town. When we pulled up our flight leader spotted what looked like four small cars on a road outside of the town. We dove on them and they turned out to be horse drawn carts which we destroyed. It bothered me to have to kill horses but we had to destroy anything that moved. Back to our base, landed safely and was briefed and then lunch. Had to go back to the flight line for the possibility of another mission. Stayed there till 17:30 but it was too late to take off for another mission. Had supper and then stayed with the Mess crew for a farewell party for one of the guys who is leaving to go to the infantry in a few days. Had a nice time and then to bed.

Saturday, March 17

Went to the Mess early, ate and went upstairs to try to take a bath that I haven't had in awhile, but no hot water. Went down to the field to pick up a Jeep that I need for the rest of the day for our move to the new field. Came back and supervised the loading of a flat bed truck that was going to take some of our equipment.

Finished loading by 13:30 and I took off in my Jeep with three of the boys who worked in the kitchen. Arrived at our new field around 3:00 and what a sight it was.

The runway is a sloping affair that is 40 ft. higher at one end then the other and the runway is a dirt strip so that if we get rain it will probably be a muddy mess. The only nice area is the living area. Spent the whole afternoon looking over the camp to see what kind of work we might have to do, and then left to go back to our base and had supper. Made plans with the Mess Sgt. for the move tomorrow with the rest of our equipment. Had a beer and a bull session at the bar and then to bed.

Sunday, March 18

Up early, had breakfast and then back to the tent to get my stuff together in preparation for the move. Went back to the Mess and all the waitresses came to me and told me they wanted to move with us to the new base. I explained to them that it was not possible and they were all very disappointed.

Went to the field and made the arrangements for the trucks for today and tomorrow and then came back and saw our advance party off. Gave them all the instructions on how to set up the new place and just hope they do it right. Had to borrow a Razor to shave because my bag had disappeared. After lunch I had to find out how I could send a cable home because I had been so busy that I had not written in 10 days. Have to get my message written in French to be able to send it and it will be changed to English on arrival. Jimmy Reece and I went to the field where I picked up a personel carrier that we are going to use to move the final bit of equipment tomorrow. Left it at the Mess Hall and then we went to a nearby town, Bar Le Duc and just walked around for awhile. Back to the base, supper and checked the final arrangements for tomorrow and to the sack.

Monday, March 19

Was awakened by the crew that was getting ready to take our tent. Got up "toute suite" and packed like mad. In a half hour had our stuff packed and the stove ready to go. Went to the Mess Hall and got the personel carrier fully loaded and ready to go. Jimmy Short threw his stuff in also, had breakfast and arranged for sandwiches and coffee to be available for all the pilots and we were finally ready to go. Our staff of waitresses kissed us all goodby and we were off. Arrived at the new base before 18:00 just in time for supper. Everything is pretty well set up but we still have beaucoup work to do. Went to our tent and unloaded our stuff. First thing we did was get the stove operational. Jimmy Short got permission to bunk with us so at 23:00 even though we were only half setup we hit the sack.

Tuesday, March 20

Up early and at the Mess Hall by 9:00 and then went to the supply area to get lumber so that the men in the Mess could go to work building tables and racks for the cooking utensils. Had some more gravel brought to the Mess area to make it more presentable. After lunch Jimmy took the truck to a nearby town and managed to get folding chairs for the Mess Hall and little café tables for the club. Everyone was very busy so I spent most of the afternoon painting the tables and they look very nice when finished. Late afternoon Jimmy went to a nearby brewery and got 150 bottles of beer and some ice so that by 17:00 the bar and club were operational. Had supper, and we are still eating out of mess kits because we only have 4 men working the Mess Hall. Nobody seems to mind because they say the food is good. At 19:30 we all went to the Group Theatre (which is a tarpaper building that was here) and saw an excellent training film on "enemy interrogation" and pictures of the invasion at Normandy.

Then to the sack!

Wednesday, March 21

It rained most of the night and was still raining this morning. After breakfast took a truck into Toul and picked up part of a whiskey ration and 7 people to work for us in the Mess area. The whiskey was not enough to be equally shared so we put it for sale at the bar. Four of the 7 men decided they did not want to live in the camp so after lunch we sent them back to town. Got cots and blankets for the other 3, got them set up and fed them and then put them to work hauling gravel to the Mess area. Picked up a tent and had the men set it up, put floorboards in it and set up an area to be able to wash dishes. Got our dishes and silverware unpacked and to be used tomorrow. Had supper and then Reasman, Jimmy and I scrounged beaucoup lumber and went to work on a floor for our tent. After 2 ½ hours we had a nice wood floor, moved our stuff into the tent and finally hit the sack.

Thursday, March 22

Up at 7:30, had breakfast and Jimmy and I went to the Club tent and lit the stove. Walked to the flight line and got myself put on a mission early this afternoon. Went back to the Mess to make sure everything was OK. Had lunch and back to the flight line at 12:15, was briefed and we took off at 13:15. Our target area was a recco along the Rhine River.

The first time around the route we did not find anything so we went around again and finally saw some enemy trucks parked in the woods. We dove on them, strafed them and dropped bombs and left several of them burning. Headed home and landed at 15:30, was interrogated and had coffee and donuts served by the Red Cross gals.

Had dinner and at 19:00 we had a meeting at which we were told about all the educational possibilities that were open to us when the war ended. After the meeting we picked up some more lumber and put it in our tent for future use and then spent time catching this diary up to date. In the sack at 23:30.

Friday, March 23

Up early, 4:45 to fly my 73rd mission. Breakfast and then to the flight line to be briefed and then sat around for awhile waiting for it to get light. Took off at 6:45 and flew to our target area which was a bridge in the Rhine River valley. When we got there we found three trains waiting to cross the bridge. Flight leader lined us up for a bombing run on the trains and then we did a strafing run on them also. As we pulled up we spotted a cart and a truck so my wingman and I dove on them and killed a German and his oxen and my wingman got the truck. Headed home, landed, was interrogated and had lunch. After lunch Jimmy and I took a jeep and went into St. Dizier. Arrived there at 14:15 and took care of the payroll for the people who work for us. Spent the rest of the time there walking around town, which was in pretty good shape. Got something in my eye so we decided to head back to base. When we got back I could hardly see out of my left eye so grabbed a quick bite and went to see Doc. He bathed my eye with some kind of solution and put salve in it and told me to see him tomorrow before flying again. In the sack at 23:00.

Saturday, March 24

Up early, had breakfast and went to see Doc to get my eye treated. It feels pretty good and I could see OK and Doc said it looks a lot better and he treated it. Got Jimmy and Reasman and went back to the tent and started work on it.

We are putting up sideboards to make it more roomy and comfortable. It took us till lunchtime to do only one side. After lunch we went back to work again.

Today is nice and warm so we were able to strip to the waist. Our squadron was stood down for the day so this place really looks like a camp in the states. Fellows are lounging around on blankets and some are playing volley ball. By 18:00 we were finished and we now have a nice wood floor, sideboards and a door on our tent, almost like home. Went to supper and sat around listening to the radio till about 21:00. Back to the tent and made some French-fried potatos and fried eggs. Doc L. came in so I whipped him up an egg, toute suite. It was lights out at 23:00

Sunday, March 25

Up early and went to breakfast to find that two of our French KP's quit this morning so we had quite a bottleneck in the dish and pot washing dept. Finally got things straightened out and Dusty and I went to Toul to draw our PX rations and came back and unpacked them. At 11:00 there was a meeting in the club for all the administrative officers in the group. It was more or less a pep rally and a chance to do whatever "bitching" we wanted to do about the Mess. We finally decided to transfer a few of our men and get some new cooks to replace them. Meeting broke up and we gave out PX rations. After lunch Jimmy and I went to see Major Chairs about the Mess set-up and we decided on a few changes. Stopped at the Dentist office on the way back and he found a few small cavities which he fixed in 15 minutes. Later borrowed a jeep and went to take a "wonderful hot shower". After supper attended a Pilot meeting which turned out to be a bull session giving everyone a chance to vent a little. Back to the tent and wrote a few letters, brought this diary up to date and to bed.

Monday, March 26   [Morty's Birthday]

At 02:00 this morning, Morty's army, the 7th is crossing the Rhine. Good Luck.

Up early and after breakfast took care of some details at the club. Off to Nancy at 10:00 and stopped at Vezelise to clear some paper work at the Finance Office. Got to Nancy at 11:30 and sent a cablegram home. Went to PX and got a new pair of combat shoes and gloves. Walked around town and bought a few souvenirs and then to the Hotel Theirs for lunch and then back to the base.

Dusty had picked up some beer coupons so we went to the brewery at Vezelise and purchased 480 bottles of beer for the club. Came back and I took care of the books for the club and then had supper and listened to the radio for awhile. Got some eggs, bread and butter and a bunch of the guys came back to our tent and we had egg sandwiches and a "bull" session.

Looking around at our gang I couldn't help but notice the change that has occurred in most of the guys now that we know the war is almost over. We know the score and we are tired, anxious to get through the next little while and want to get home. This war really isn't much fun anymore.

Tuesday, March 27 ----My Birthday

Up at 6:45 because I was scheduled for a mission. Today being my birthday doesn't make the day any different at all. Had breakfast and went to the flight line and was briefed for a 11:30 mission. Most of our mission today was to patrol over the 3rd Army bridgehead giving them protective air cover, but the weather was so bad that we would not have been able to get over 3000 ft so at 10:00 the mission was called off.

A few of us went over to one of the crew chiefs tent and sat around listening to his phonograph. After lunch went back to the flight line. Two missions had taken off but the weather turned very bad and they had to turn back and land in heavy rain. One of the other pilots and I took a couple of jeeps to run a taxi service to get the pilots from their planes back to the Operations tent. After supper a bunch of the guys came back to our tent and we finished off the two dozen eggs that were left over from breakfast and I had saved. Into the sack at 23:30.

Wednesday, March 28

Up at 07:45 to find the weather miserable again. After breakfast gathered some laundry and dry cleaning stuff together and three of the guys and I drove into Nancy which is only 15 miles away. Left my stuff to be cleaned and then to the PX to buy a few odds and ends. Roamed around town for awhile and then we went to the Air Corps Hotel for lunch. Had a swell meal and then decided to return to the base because the weather looked like it was going to clear up and we might be able to fly. Got back but nothing was scheduled. Took the time to go through my log book and found that I have 185 hours of combat flying time.

Went to see Major Andres, our Squadron CO and asked him if I could possibly go home on a 30 day leave and he said yes, that it was possible but not for about a month. He said he would speak to the Col. And let me know. Went to supper and picked up my mail and there was beaucoup of it.

Finally received Morty's address so I went over to Ops to get some help in locating his outfit, but no one was there, so it will have to wait.

Reece came back from Lyon today and he had a great time We went to the movie and saw "Ministry Of Fear" which was excellent. Got back to the tent and read Judy's letters till after midnight and could hardly keep my eyes open.

Thursday, March 29

Up early and heard the rain on the tent so I turned over and did not get up till 10:00. Sat around the warm stove till noon and then we all went to eat. After lunch checked in the extra ration we had received for the pilots. It consists of 3 packs of jam, 3 candy bars, 3 apples and 3 eggs per pilot each week. Went to report to the Col. And he ordered the rations to be given out except for the eggs which he wants to be served at breakfast. Also asked him if I could take a few days off to go to see my brother and he said yes. Went to Ops and the Air Liason Officer located Morty's outfit for me and gave me a road map to help. Made arrangement for a Jeep and got a pass for Dusty to come with me. Took a personel carrier down to pick up a load of beer. Had supper and then gave out the special pilots ration. Went back to the tent and spent the rest of the evening reading and rereading all the mail I had received and then to bed.

Friday, March 30

Awoke at 6:30 and went to get the Jeep that I would be using. Rolled up my sack and put it in the Jeep. Had breakfast and Dusty threw his stuff in the Jeep and we took off for the front lines. Went through Nancy, Luneville, Saarburg, Saverne, Hageman and Wisemberg where I finally found the 6th Corps headquarters. As we got nearer the front lines each town was more beat up. At 6th Corps we were able to have lunch in their Officers Mess and then I got the information about where Morty's outfit might be.

Went to the town where his outfit was supposed to be but they had already moved on. Got gas for the Jeep and headed for Ludwigshafen where his outfit was supposed to be. Arrived there at 17:00 and this town had really taken a pounding. There isn't a whole house standing anywhere. Finally found his outfit and stopped a GI and asked if he knew where I might find Morty.

He asked who I was and when I told him that I was Morty's brother he said he was sorry to tell me that he had been wounded. When he told me that, I felt as if a hand was squeezing my heart. Found the 1st Sgt. and he took me to the office they had set up and looked in the records and found that Morty had been wounded on, March 20 with mortar shells to the chest and leg and was listed as "seriously wounded", but they assured me that he was OK. The fellow who had picked him up told me the whole story.

They were on a hill near the Siegfried Line when the Krauts opened up on them with a mortar. Morty got hit by some of the shrapnel and he was taken to the aid station immediately and he never lost consciousness. They said he was "a good soldier" and I felt proud of him. They shared some of their food with us and then directed me to the aid station. Went there and found out that he had been sent to the 11th Field Hospital. It was pretty late so we decided to stay with them tonite. Bought our sacks in and sat around listening to their war stories.They showed us guns, knives and other odds and ends that they had taken as souvenirs. In Germany they just take what they want.

Saturday, March 31

Awoke at 6:45 packed our stuff in the jeep and they took us to the Officers Mess, which was pretty good. Had breakfast and said our goodbyes and thanked them for their help and we took off. Went back to Landau to the 6th Corps Hdq. again and found that they had moved up to Mannhein very early this morning. Managed to find out where the 11th Evac Hospital was and we took off for it. Arrived there at 12:45 to find that they were moving also. Spoke to one surgeon who remembered Morty's name and he told me that he had been sent to the Nancy area on a hospital train on, March 25th. Got a bite to eat and took off for Nancy at 13:30. Had to stop at an emergency service station at a motor pool to get a flat fixed on the Jeep. Finally got to Nancy at 17:45 and parked the Jeep in a M.P. lot went to the Hotel Thiers and ate. From there went over to Conrad (Continental Advanced) and went up to the Medical Section. Met a Major Berman and Capt. Horowitz and explained that I was trying to find my brother who had been wounded. They were really swell and they spent nearly an hour hunting through files and making phone calls till they finally found that he was in a Hospital only 40 miles from where my airbase was. I thanked them and Dusty and I took off for our camp. Got back at 20:30 and showed the boys our souvenirs and told about the trip and then hit the sack.

Chapter 10 – April 1945

Sunday, April 1

Up at 8:00, had breakfast and then made plans with Jimmy about what had to be done today and then went down to Ops and looked up Vittel on the map. That is where the Hospital is that Morty is in. Took off at 10:00 and was there by 11:00. Went to the registrars office and found Morty's ward . A nurse took me to the ward and went in to tell him he had a visitor. When he saw me I thought he was going to jump out of bed. We were both so excited and after a big hug we both started talking. At noon they brought his lunch and a tray for me. We ate and talked all afternoon. Wrote a letter home which, as an officer I censored. Finally at 16:00 I left and went back to my field and checked to make sure that everything was ready for the birthday party for everyone whose birthday was in March. Had dinner with a little champagne from the party, back to the tent and read more mail and then to the sack. Had to turn our watches ahead one hour tonight.

Monday, April 2

Awoke at 8:00, shaved, washed, dressed and brought this diary up to date. Had breakfast and checked that everything was OK in the Mess Hall. The advance party left for our new field in Germany this morning, but we do not know when we are moving. After lunch came back to the tent and prepared some things to take to Morty.

Reasman was not flying today so he decided to come to the hospital with me. Got to the hospital at 1:45. Morty was feeling better today, Told me that the Dr. was going to sew up his leg this morning but it looked so good that he only taped it. Stayed a few hours and we got back to base in time for supper. After supper got gas for our stove and then returned the jeep to the motor pool. Stopped at the club tent and borrowed a typewriter and then back to the tent and typed lots of letters home and then hit the sack.

Tuesday, April 3

Awoke late because it had been storming all night. Made some toasted cheese sandwiched for breakfast and then went to the Mess tent to make sure there was nothing I had to take care of. After lunch met with a couple of the boys and we made plans to go hunting because there were no missions scheduled. Borrowed Dusty's carbine and went to the line to pick up ammunition and went a nearby wooded area to look for targets. Had no luck so came back and grabbed a quick bite and went back to the woods again. We disbursed ourselves around a stream and waited for some deer to show up, but none of them did. One rabbit crossed the field and I took a shot it and missed. On the way back we shot at a few more rabbits and missed again. Our jeep must have looked like a tank with all the guns sticking out of it. Got back around 22:00 and bat the breeze for awhile and hit the sack early.

Wednesday, April 4

Up early, washed, dressed went to the Mess and had breakfast and then got a few things together to take to Morty. I was on a late mission today so my morning was free. On the way to the hospital the ignition wire on the jeep broke but I was able to get into an Army Motor Pool and they fixed it for me.

Got to the hospital around 10:30 and spent time with Morty and left to get back to the field because I had a mission at mid afternoon. Morty is taking things easy and he seems to be getting along OK.

Briefed for the mission which was going to be a recon with no specific target. Took off at 16:00, crossed the bomb line and started our recon. Our flight leader brought us over a rail yard which appeared to be empty and we dove on it and dropped our bombs on the tracks. Got back in formation and spotted a long column of troops, Marching on a road and when we dove on them we saw that they were American POW's. We made one pass over the column to see if we could scare off the German guards, but nothing happened. Flew over them and they were waving at us and we left. Landed at 19:15 and was interrogated and then to supper. Listened to the radio for awhile, wrote a few letters and then hit the sack.

Thursday, April 5

Up at 7:30 and went to the Mess Hall to find out that our Mess truck turned over last night returning from St. Dizier but luckily nobody was hurt. The truck is a complete loss just when we need it most for our upcoming move. Filled out the necessary papers on the accident and turned them in. Went to see Lt. Hunt to get the particulars from him concerning our upcoming move to Germany. Got Tokarz and Dusty together to give them the poop about the move and we did a little planning. Had lunch and took care of a few more details and one of the fellows and I drove down to Vezelise to take a shower but it wasn't open yet.

Went back to camp and arranged for all our rented chairs and tables to be returned and then back to Vezelise to get into that great hot shower, I hated to get out.

Back to camp at 17:30 where there were only about 30 Officers left to be served so we had a magnificent steak for supper. After supper the trucks came so we loaded the Mess and part of the Officers club in the next two hours. Had a few drinks and then hit the sack.

Friday, April 6

My alarm went off at 5:00. Got up and went to the enlisted men mess for breakfast and then got together with all my boys working to load all the trucks by 6:30. Took down the tents and threw them on the trucks also and they all took off in the trucks except the 6 of them who were going in the B-25. Took some baggage to the plane and Tokarz went with it on the plane. Took 5 of the guys back to police the area and burn up all the trash and a short while later the B-25 returned and they then took off for the new base. Kibitzed with Lt. Hunt for awhile and then we went to the enlisted mess again and had another terrific steak. After lunch I sent Dusty down to the Labor office to turn in the time sheets so that our civilian workers would be paid and he also returned all the empty beer bottles to the brewery. Dusty got back at 15:00 and we took off for Nancy to pick up our dry cleaning and laundry and back to camp to pack up the rest of our stuff. Had some more of that great steak and potatos for supper. Having a small mess like this is great. After eating moved my personal stuff to dusty"s tent and then loaded the Personel Carrier so that we could get an early start in the morning. Listened to the news and then hit the sack.

Saturday, April 7

Awoke at 7:00, had breakfast, finished loading the truck and took down the tent and threw it on top of the load and took off at 9:00.

Had been traveling about two hours when we got a flat tire. Couldn't find a jack and while we were debating what to do along came a convoy of trucks from our group. Stopped them and borrowed a jack and got the tire changed. Took off and made it to the Continental Advanced Section for some lunch. Their setup is really good. You turn in some rations to them and in return they serve you a hot meal.

Set off again and we finally reached the Rhine River at 17:00. I really got a thrill driving across the pontoon bridge, knowing that only two weeks before the engineers had fought to clear the area and put up the bridge. Arrived at our new base about 18:30 and it looks great. We have a very long building for our Club and Mess and our tents are set up in a pine grove. Unloaded the truck and then I found the tent that Reasman and Reece had set up for us. Got my stuff unloaded and hit the sack early.

Sunday, April 8

Slept late till 9:00 and went to the Mess and got all the cooks together to tell them that the shifts were being changed and that from now on they had to work every other day instead of every third. They didn't like it but "c'est le guerre" After that I went to headquarters and spoke to Major Chairs about switching some of the cooks back to the squadron and give us new men to replace them.

Finally got that settled and came back, had lunch and got the kitchen crew working on setting up the tables and cleaning the dishes and got Dusty, Joe and Mike to build a bar. We put up rows of thin bamboo all along the walls and over the front and side of the bar and then I went down to the 57th Service Gp. and got some paint and brushes and we painted the bar which looked pretty snazzy.

Ate supper and then Jimmy got back with 12 cases of Benedictine and Brandy and chairs and tables that he had "liberated". Opened the bar for awhile but had to close down at 21:00 because there is a blackout in force around here. Hit the sack early.

Monday, April 9

Woke at 9:00 because my alarm failed to go off. Had a few eggs and got to the club at ten and had to get Jimmy and the boys going. Then went to the dispensary to see Doc who has been giving me radium treatments. He checked me out and everything is OK. Went to Supply to get light bulbs for the Mess and came back and started the boys painting our chairs and tables, red, yellow and blue. Had lunch and finally we finished the painting by 14:00. It all looks lively and colorful. Dusty and I went to the Service Group and drew the PX ration for the Officers. Got back by 17:00 and got everything unpacked and distributed and finished by 19:00. Ate supper and then Reasman and I had a drink and played darts for awhile. Wrote letter and hit the sack at 23:00.

Tuesday, April 10

Awoke at 4:30 when I heard them come for Reasman for a mission and then slept till 9:00. Got up and had breakfast and got Jimmy out of the sack and setup and to Headquarters to check on a few things. When I got back I found that the Service Group had sent over a lot of confiscated German foodstuffs. There were cans of Kosher pickles, relish and pickled beets and everything was delicious. Did a lot of tasting so I had no appetite for lunch. Helped the boys put a metal top on the bar and then Dusty and I went to the Service Group to pickup more rations.

Came back and Jimmy challenged me to a ping pong game and he won two out of three .Had supper and a drink at the bar and came back to the tent. Was reading the Readers Digest when suddenly the ack-ack guns all around the field started shooting. Turned out all the lights and went outside and saw a beautiful display of fireworks. Things finally quieted down and hit the sack.

Wednesday, April 11

Was awakened at 4:30 for a mission. Had breakfast and went to be briefed for a recco mission looking for "targets of opportunity". Once we got over enemy territory we spotted trains that were moving and for the next ½ hour we were very busy strafing them. Scored lots of hits. Came back and landed at 9:00, was interrogated and we reported 2 trains destroyed and three that were damaged. Went to the Mess and found that Tokarz had drawn another supply of the extra rations for pilots so I called the Ops and told them to pass the word and send the guys up for their ration. Had lunch, then showered and went over to the Service Group to scrounge some more of the pickles, relish and beets.

After supper went to see Major Chairs about my request for a thirty day leave to go home. He said he would check with the Col. Came back to the tent, brought this diary up to date and was told about the 441st Troop Carrier Squadron that had sent their orchestra to our field today to entertain in appreciation for the fine escort our group had given them the day before..

Thursday, April 12

Awoke at 7:30 and had breakfast and went to headquarters and was told that we had two new stoves coming for our Mess. Told Tokarz to pick them up and then went down to the line. I am on the second mission today, but the first mission was still standing by because of bad weather. Went back to the Mess Hall, wrote some letters, ate lunch and then went back to the flight line. My plane had come back from a mission all shot up so it has to go to the Service Grp. for repairs. I made arrangements with our squadron painter to paint the name on it after the repairs are done. Hung around the ready area till 15:00 when we finally briefed for the second mission of the day. It was going to be a mission of 24 planes to bomb gun positions at Nurenburg. We took off at 16:15 and made our way up through the clouds, climbing all the time. As we approached the target area the number two man in the flight started having trouble with his plane so the flight leader told me to escort him back to the field. Heading back we got separated in a bank off clouds so we each called the controller for bearings and both landed safely back at the field. It was raining when we were landing but we made it OK. After supper went to a movie that was showing. It was a Bing Crosby film. Went to the club, had a drink, and home and hit the sack.

Friday, April 13

Awake at 7:30 when the alarm went off, but the weather was bad so I dozed off again. Up at nine and we were told to go the flight line after breakfast. We were put on standby because of bad weather. Borrowed a bicycle and rode over to the Service Sq. to see how the repairs on my plane were coming along. It will be five more days before it will be ready to fly again.

Had lunch and reported back to the line. At 1:30 we were finally told to stand by in our quarters because the weather was so bad. A few of us decided to take a chance on us not flying and decided to go on a scrounging party. We went to the Adler Automobile factory in Frankfurt. The place must have been a honey at one time. Most of the machinery looked brand new and there seemed to be plenty of material to be worked on. We went through the basement and first floor and looked through lots of cabinets and much to my surprise found lots of fine precision gauges and measuring instruments.

Because of my training as a tool and die maker before I went into service I realized the value of this equipment so I collected a lot of them. After seeing that factory it is easier to understand why the Germans have been able to fight for so long. Finally went back to camp, had supper, read my mail and hit the sack. Friday the 13th had not been so unlucky.

Saturday, April 14

Awakened at 5:30 for a mission, got up, ate and went to the line and we were briefed for our mission which was a recce to look for targets of opportunity. Had to stand by because of heavy ground fog. Finally took off at 10:45 and headed into Germany. The weather was pretty bad and we could not see much because of the clouds so the controller directed us to bomb the town of Ludwigsburg. Bombed and caught very heavy flak but luckily no one was hit.

Landed at 13:00, was interrogated and had lunch. Checked with Jimmy to see what he had brought back from Trier. He had somehow found bottles of champagne and sparkling burgundy.

At 15:30 went back to the line and was briefed and took off on a mission at 17:30. Flew over our recce route twice and could not find a target, but on the way home we spotted some boxcars in a rail yard and after strafing them we left them burning and we headed home. Was interrogated, had dinner and then went to the club where we found out that we were stood down tomorrow so everyone was at the bar having a great time. Everyone got a little drunk and it was a wild party and was still going strong when I left at 23:00. Read my mail and hit the sack.

Sunday, April 15

Set a record, slept till after 11:00, the latest I've slept since I   have been overseas. Got up, dressed, shaved and went to eat. After eating met Reasman and we borrowed a Jeep and went over to the 57th Service Group and just shot the bull with Capt. Marks for awhile. Came back at 14:30, had some coffee at the Red Cross shack and then watched a ball game for awhile. The enlisted men skunked the officers 18 to 2. Went to the dentist at 15:45 to have a cavity filled were I had lost the filling. Came back to the club and everyone was excited about the news that there was a rumor that Hitler and his Generals want to capitulate and it seems too good to be true. Had to go to a Pilots meeting at the flight line where we reviewed our gun camera films and then we saw pictures that had been taken of the new German Jet Fighters so that we would know what they looked like and what they were capable of doing. After supper I went to the club because they were having trouble with the generator and the lights were not working. Finally got everything fixed and went to our tent. Wrote some letters and hit the sack.

Monday, April 16

Awoke at 4:30 when they got some of the pilots up for the early mission and the dozed off till 9:00. Up and dressed, had breakfast and went to the flight line and saw that I was scheduled for a mission at 14:00. Went to the Service Gp. With a couple of the guys to get a much needed haircut and shot the bull with Capt Marks while I waited for the rest of the guys to get their haircuts.

Got back and had lunch and then went to be briefed for our mission. Again it was a recce to find whatever targets we could. Took off at 14:00 and right after we crossed the bomb line we found a column of German trucks which we dove on and strafed. Destroyed two of the trucks and left the others damaged. Continued our patrol but did not find any other targets so headed home and landed at 17:00. All the time that we had been up we had received warnings to watch for enemy planes that had been sighted in our area, but we never saw any of them.

Was interrogated, picked up some mail that had come for me, ate and then borrowed a Jeep and went to the gas dump to get some gas for our stove. Back to the tent and hit the sack early because I am on the first mission tomorrow.

Tuesday, April 17

Was awakened at 6:30 for the mission. Had breakfast and went to the flight line to be briefed. Took off and the mission again was a recce because there are not a lot of targets left for us to go after. We caught three trains in a rail yard in German territory and dive bombed them and saw that we got direct hits and destroyed all of them.

There was a hospital near the tracks that might have suffered some damage also. We then found a small German airfield and there were 4 planes parked in the trees around the edge of the field and we strafed and destroyed them. My wingman called that he was having trouble with his plane so the flight leader told me to escort him back to our field.

Landed OK and was interrogated and had lunch. After lunch went over to Steve's tent to pick up some of the brilliant red cloth that he had picked up somewhere and took it to our parachute maintenance man to make a scarf for me. Briefed for another mission at 14:15 and then took off on another recce.

Right after we crossed the bomb line we spotted a group of armored cars headed down a tree lined road. Dive bombed and strafed and destroyed all of them. Headed back and landed by 18:15 and was interrogated and went to supper which was delicious fried chicken. Was told that some of our Polish kitchen workers had been goofing of so Tokarz and I got them together to lay the law down. Back to my tent and in the sack at 23:00.

Wednesday, April 18

Up at 7:45, ate and went to Steve's tent to check the motorcycle he had picked up. It is simple to operate and after he showed me what to do he let me take it for a ride. It was more fun then I had in a long time. Steve had to leave so he told me to keep the bike till he got back. Went to the flight line and at 10:30 we were briefed for a mission. This was a big one. It was a group mission of 48 planes. We were to hit three airfields and then provide cover for the medium bombers that were going to follow us in and hit other targets.

We took off at 11:45 and hit our targets OK but there was heavy ack ack and the Col. who was leading the group got hit by the anti-aircraft fire and his plane was badly damaged. We all headed home and found out that the Col. had to belly land his plane about 20 miles inside the bomb line but he was recovered and is OK.

Were interrogated, had lunch and then Reece and I took the motorcycle to go to take a shower and then had fun riding the motorcycle around the field. Had dinner and came out to find the bike with a flat so we took the wheel off and went to the motor pool and patched the tube, fixed it back on the bike and returned it to Steve. Played some ping pong with Jimmy and hit the sack at 23:00

Thursday, April 19

Alarm went off at 7:30 but dozed off again till 9:00. Ate and then got Steve and we took off on a scrounging party at 10:30. It was a long dusty ride to Heilbrunn and got there about noon. We stopped at what had been a insignia factory and found a motorcycle which we put in the weapons carrier that we were using today. Went through the factory and found beaucoup insignia that became our souvenirs. From there we went to another small factory because Steve was looking to find a bicycle, but no luck. We came to what looked like a stationary store and Steve found a bike in the back of the store.

Rode around town to see what else we could find. This town was pretty beat up. Came to what had been a brewery and Steve found another bike which was added to what we already had in the truck. Finally left for home and arrived back at 19:00 and had supper.

Got one of the mechanics to complete the repairs on the motorcycle and then went to a Pilots meeting, but not much happened there. Lots of speculation about how close we were to the war ending. Took my motorcycle to the Mess Hall and parked it for the night and back to our tent, wrote some letters and hit the sack.

Friday, April 20

Was awakened at 4:30 for a mission. Got up, ate and went to be briefed. We took off as soon as it was light and we flew a very uneventful mission and landed back at the field at 9:00, was interrogated, had some Red Cross coffee and donuts and were briefed for our next mission which will be at 1:00. We took off and flew to the Stuttgart area where it was reported that there was a large movement of enemy vehicles. When we got there we found that the report was correct and there were beaucoup vehicles on the road and also parked. Our flight leader had us split into two ship elements and we were each given different area and we went to work. My area was full of parked trucks and some horse drawn carts and my wingman and I accounted for destroying 15 of them. When we finally left the entire area was burning and nothing was moving. Landed at 12:30, was interrogated and had lunch. Got my motorcycle and rode around for awhile but it still need some tuning up so made arrangements to bring it in tomorrow. Had supper and then Reasman and I rode around on the bike again. Back to the tent, wrote letters and hit the sack.

Saturday, April 21

Awoke at 7:45, dressed, had breakfast and took my motorcycle down to the flight line for my crew chief and one of the other men to work on it. Before I left they had the whole bike apart.

Had to leave at 11:30 in time to eat and be briefed for a mission.

We took off at 13:15 to fly a recce and look for possible targets. After an uneventful 2 and ½ hours and no luck finding anything we came back and landed. When we returned we found an A-26 Group had been forced to land at our field because of bad weather. After we were interrogated and we started talking to the pilots from the group I found a pilot that I had gone through training with as a Cadet. We shot the breeze for awhile exchanging war stories.

Went to the Orderly room to send home some of my last pay and then to the Mess for supper. After supper I could see that we were in for a long evening because there were about 40 pilots from that outfit mixing with our group and the bar was doing a great business. In our squadron Reasman and nine other officers had just received their First Lieutenant promotion and they were celebrating also and they celebrated so much that we had to take Reasman home and put him to bed at 22:00.

Sunday, April 22

Awoke at 8:30, dressed went to the Mess and then to the flight line to be briefed for a mission. Sat around listening to the radio until 10:00 when we were finally briefed went to our planes and took off for a mission to bomb a reported concentration of trucks. The weather is miserable and we finally fought our way through the clouds and when we got out on top we were at 18000 feet and we could not see the ground. Our fight leader called the controller and he gave us an "egg basket". That is were he vectored us over a target area and told us when to drop our bombs. Came back and dropped through the clouds and safely landed and was briefed.

Went to the club and sat by the stove writing letters. At 18:00 took our weapons carrier over to the Motor Pool to have some repairs taken care of and then had supper. Made arrangements for another scrounging trip tomorrow. Finally in the sack around 23:00.

Monday, April 23

Up at 7:30 went and had breakfast and made arrangements for the truck and a box of food and came back to the tent, washed and shaved and got ready to go. Finally around 10:00 four of us took off to go to Stuttgart which had just been taken by the French Army yesterday. Nearly every town we went through was terribly beat up. We all were glad that Germany finally got a taste of the war also. It is not only the cities in Germany that are getting destroyed but every little town is feeling the war. When we got to Stuttgart the boys were really ready to do our scrounging. We found some wine, liquor and champagne in a bombed out café and then we started going through stores on the main drag. Found a few odds and ends and finally came to the Zeiss-Ikon camera factory. It was interesting that the factory had not been damaged at all and there were still two German guards there. Went through looking for cameras but there weren't any. We stopped at what had been a local police station and found some beautiful swords, guns, binoculars and knives. Finally left Stuttgart at 19:00 and arrived back in camp at 22:00. Unloaded the truck and had a bite to eat and by the time I got everything straightened out it was midnight.

Tuesday, April 24

Awakened at 4:30 for a mission. Got up,splashed some water on my face to wake me up, went to eat and to the flight line to be briefed. Took off at 7:20 to find targets of opportunity. When we got to our recce area we spotted three trains just leaving a rail yard. We dove on then and blew them up and nice to see that we left them burning. From there our flight leader spotted a nearby airfield with 10 Jet planes at the end of a runway so half of our flight bombed and strafed them while the rest of the flight provided protective cover. They destroyed two and damaged 8 of the planes. We then discovered ME109's parked around all the edges of the field and we proceeded to strafe and bomb. We made 6 passes around the field and when we finished we confirmed 21 planes destroyed and at least 14 more damaged. I blew up 2 of the ME's and damaged three of them myself.

By then we were getting low on gas so we had to get back in formation and head home. We landed and were interrogated and at 10:45 briefed for another mission and took off again at 11:45. It was another recce in a different area and we did not find any targets so we landed back at the field at 14:30, was interrogated and then to lunch.

After lunch the rest of my day was free so I stopped at Headquarters and chewed the fat for awhile and then back to make sure everything was OK at the Mess and had supper and back to my tent. Doc Lowenstein came over to look at my souvenir collection and stayed for about an hour. Brought this diary up to date and hit the sack at 23:00

Wednesday, April 25

Alarm went off at 7:15, but dozed off again and did not get up until10:00. Dressed, shaved went to the Mess and had a bite and nothing was doing there so I went to the flight line. Our first mission did not take off till 11:00 this morning, which was very unusual. Went back to the Mess and had lunch and then went over to the Special Service area where they had a band giving a concert.

Stayed there for awhile enjoying the music and went back to the flight line where I was scheduled for a mission. Wrote a few letters and was briefed at 14:00 and we took off at 15:00. Again the mission was a recce and after flying for an hour all we found was a moving train and we dove on it and clobbered the locomotive. We continued covering the area that we had been sent to and found a small airfield loaded with many different kinds of planes. We made 5 passes at the field and destroyed 21 of the planes and left a few damaged. Had to head home because gas was getting low. After landing was interrogated and then went to supper. After eating Steve and I went to the movies and saw a terrific "Thin Man" movie. Stopped at the club and nothing was doing there so went back to the tent and chewed the fat with the boys and hit the sack.

Thursday, April 26

Slept late and did not get up till 11:00. Washed, dressed and had some cheese and crackers and after lunch went to the carpenters tent to ask him to make a box for me to send some of the souvenirs home. Stopped on the way back and talked to one of the fellows who had just returned from a leave in England.

He said that all of the 8th Air Force heavy bomber groups are packing up and preparing to leave for home and then the Pacific. Around our group we can feel the tension because everyone is waiting for the war to end so that we will find out what will be happening with us. Reasman now has 101 missions and he spoke to Capt. Young today about going home. Capt. Young told him that he will have to keep on flying till the war ends. What a load of crap that is.

Nothing much was going on so I went to where they were showing a movie and partway through the machine broke down.

Came back to the Mess and borrowed the truck and went to take a shower. Boy, it felt good to clean up. Came back to Mess, picked up some mail and a bottle of champagne and went back to the tent where we finished off the bottle and hit the sack.

Friday, April 27

Was awakened at 7:00 for a mission. Washed, dressed, had breakfast and went to the flight line to be briefed. We had to stand by for awhile but we finally took off at 9:30. When we got to the front lines the controller reported the location of an enemy ammunition dump which they ordered us to bomb. Located the dump and two of our four planes were told to bomb the dump, which they did and we all saw it blow up.

Continued on our recce and spotted a train leaving a station and the flight leader told me and my wingman to strafe the train, which we did and left it on fire. Continued our patrol and spotted a group of tanks and trucks at the edge of some woods. We dived on them and strafed them leaving all the trucks on fire. I caught one truck loaded with German troops trying to get away and strafed them and watched the truck blow up. We then had to head back to the field because our gas and ammo were both getting low. Landed at 12:30, was interrogated and had lunch.

After lunch they were showing a movie called Casanova Brown with Gary Cooper which I watched because I didn't have another mission till 16:30. Came back to the Mess, ate and went down to Ops.even though it was raining. We started to brief for a mission but the weather turned so bad that all flying was called off.

Listened to the radio for awhile and then a Pilots Meeting was called and we all got the bad news that even though it looks like the war is ending we still have to keep flying our missions. Came back to the tent and hit the sack at 23:00

Saturday, April 28

Awoke at 7:00 when the alarm went off but dozed off again because the weather is terrible. It is a perfect day for sleeping. Finally got up and dressed and went to the Mess Hall and hung around because I didn't have anything else to do. I was officially notified that I am finally being relieved of my job as Club Officer but I still have to take care of the darn Mess Hall. After lunch went to Ops and found that everything was on standby because of the bad weather. Talked to our C.O. about Reasman and I getting the OK to go to rest camp and spoke to Doc about it also but did not get an answer. Came back to the Club and picked up some candy and went to the movies again. After the movie came back to the club and listened to the radio till supper. After supper went to have Doc look at a rash that was on my legs. He painted and gave me some vitamin pills and then I came back to the tent and we cracked a bottle of champagne before going to bed.

Sunday, April 29

Did not get up till after 10:00 because today was a day off for our entire squadron. Washed, dressed and went to the Mess Hall. Finished a letter to Judy that I had started last night and had "brunch". After lunch we had to arrange the tables in the Mess Hall for a Court Martial that was taking place this afternoon. Got everything set and the Court Martial started at 14:00.

They tried an enlisted man who had been drunk and disorderly and had damaged some of the Army material and sentenced him to two months at hard labor and loss of half of his pay. After the trial we put the place back in shape and I went to the Service Group to pay for the liquor ration which is coming tomorrow. Picked up some gas for our stove and then Reasman and I went to play ping pong.

After supper came back to the tent and packed up some of the souvenirs I want to send home so that Jimmy can take them with him. He is going to France, where the censorship regulations are not as strict as they are here and will send them for me. Came back to the tent and finally hit the sack.

Monday, April 30

Was awakened at 4:00 for the early mission. After breakfast went to the flight line and briefed and we took off at 5:45 as it was getting light. The troops are moving so darn fast that our recce area keeps getting smaller. Got to the bomb line and we had to get down on the deck because the weather had turned bad again. We spotted a few enemy cars and trucks that we strafed and left burning and then we had to head home. Was interrogated and then just hung around the Ops tent all morning sweating out the weather. Finally went to lunch and hung around for awhile before going back to the line. Nothing was doing so a few of went to see if we could take a shower but the place was closed. Went back and finally briefed for a mission and took off at 16:00. We got halfway out on our course but the clouds were closing in so fast that we had to return to base. We got credit for the mission though so I now have 92. Ate dinner and Jimmy is now back from his trip where he was searching for souvenirs and all he had were swords and daggers. Shot the bull for awhile, wrote letters and hit the sack.

Chapter 11 – May 1945

Tuesday, May 1

Nothing much was doing, so I listened to a lecture that the Intelligence officer was giving to the new sports. Our squadron missions today are all patrols which is a good sign that we are finished over here. Everybody is sweating out what little information as to where we go next, but no one seems to know.

Played a little softball till suppertime. After chow we went out to watch a ball game on the field. The officers won 9 to 6 but it was a miracle. At 2300, the news broadcast said that Hitler was dead. That's darned good news, but now we don't know what to think., Maybe the war will end immediately or, Maybe it will drag on. We will see.

Wednesday, May 2

My Mess Sergeant was taken to the hospital this morning for what they think is appendicitis. I made arrangements for everything to run smoothly. Played ping pong until suppertime. After supper Reasman and I went to the show which was "A Tree Grows In Brooklyn." It was marvelous. Shot the bull with Captain Marks for awhile. He gave us some very disheartening rumors. He said that our outfit is slated for the C.B. I. theater. From now on, I'll say my prayers every night until something definite happens.

Thursday, May 3

Was on the early mission today but the weather was miserable, so when we got to the target area, we couldn't see a thing but turn around and come home.

That's 93 missions now. Landed and was interrogated and went to the orderly room to send Mother's Day Greetings.

On my way out, Captain Young called me and told me that I was getting a seven day leave to visit Morty instead of a regular rest leave. That suits me fine. Went to a nearby hospital to see if they could tell me where Morty was from his address, but they couldn't help me.. I went to the Conad Headquarters and who should I see there but the same Jewish Major and Captain who located Morty for me last time. They were only too glad to help, and in a few minutes I had his exact location.

Friday, May 4

This lazy life is getting me down. Checked the menu and saw that everything was O.K. and then went down to the line. Our first mission this morning had some luck and caught a convoy of SS troops and shot them up killing most of them and destroying their vehicles. The weather has been closing in, so the next mission is standing by. Hung around until 1600 when we were stood down. After eating I found out that my leave to see Morty was approved. I was told that the Group Commander wanted to see me. Hung around the club all evening, but he didn't show up.

Saturday, May 5

I spoke to our C. O. and he told me that he approved my leave, but he thought I wasn't putting in enough time on my Mess Officer job. I told him that I couldn't very well fly two missions a day as I have been doing and still take care of this place. I told him that from now on I will be able to spend more time here.

Someone had broken into the kitchen last night and messed the whole place up. I reported it to headquarters and God help the man who did it if we ever find him.

Sunday, May 6

Got an Army wrist watch from Tech Supply which I'm going to take down to Morty and then went to the service Squadron to get a snazzy leather strap for it. Came back and found that my orders are ready for whenever I want to leave. If the darn weather would clear up, I'd be able to take off.

Monday, May 7

Went out to the line and got one of the new planes to test hop. Went out and started up and was ready to go, I got a call from the tower telling me to return to the line. When I got back in, they said the runway was still too muddy to use.

The new Mess Officer came in today. I ate lunch with him and told him a lot about the job. An announcement was made at lunch today that there would be a formation at 1500 for everyone in the group. We all had to wear Class A uniform. That could only mean one thing--VICTORY. At 1430 we all went down to OPs and lined up. We then, Marched out on the field. The whole group, 1,000 men was there and it really was a great sight. At 1500, Colonel Nevitt came out and read a message he had received from 12th Air Force saying that the **war was over**.

I couldn't help getting a lump in my throat when the good news was actually announced. We were waiting so long for this wonderful day that now it is here it is so hard to believe.

Colonel Nevitt made a nice little speech and then we were all dismissed. There wasn't any cheering or yelling. Everyone walked off the field quietly and with his closest friends. When we got back to the tent area, we all gathered around and strangely enough, the talk wasn't of victory, but it was of our buddies: Bond, Young, Nane, Hack, Foster, Alworth, Banner, Kuykendal, Turner and Neilson who hadn't lived to see the victory. The colonel said, "our victory is tempered with sadness, because there are some who aren't here to share in the victory that they helped win." And he is right.

Got to my tent and packed my bag so that I'll be ready to leave tomorrow if the B-25 goes. After supper we all went out to watch the ball game. After it was over we all came back to the Club and drank a bit. I was happier than I'd been in a long time.

Tuesday, May 8

At 1500 we listened to Winston Churchill's speech. According to him, England won the war. I'm surprised that we're on such good terms with England. Got a pleasant surprise. Bob Hope, Francis Langford and Jerry Colona stopped here on their way to doing a USO show for the troops and they had lunch with us. After they left I went back to the Club and played some ping pong. Just lay around and chewed the fat until suppertime. This lazy life is swell for a change.

Wednesday, May 9

Was told we wouldn't leave for Rest Camp till tomorrow. At 1100 we all, Marched out on the field and lined up. The Chaplain read a brief prayer and then the colonel read off the list of names of all the men who had given their lives in the war.

The Chaplain said a prayer for them and then the service was over. It was a very simple service but also had been very touching. I hope that all my friends who died have not given their lives in vain. We must win a strong peace before we can really say that the war is over.

Thursday, May 10

Went down to the B-25 and at 0810 we took off. Read and dozed all the way down. At 1030, we landed at Cannes and from then on it was wonderful. Jeeps were waiting and they took us to the Hotel Martinez, an eight story cream colored building, which is gorgeous. It is right on the water's edge . It was just like being a civilian again. Bellhops came out and took our bags, and we all went out to a small reception room and registered. After eating lunch, I called Morty and told him that I am going to try to get down and see him tomorrow before he takes off on a hospital ship to go home. Ryan and I went down to the beach and got a kayak that the hotel has for its guests. We had a swell time paddling around.

Friday, May 11

After eating I called up the Rail Travel Officer and got a reservation on the train to Aix en Province this afternoon so that I could see Morty before his hospital ship took him home.

Had lunch and then went to catch the train. Made the right connections and got to see Morty and was delighted that he seemed much better and was on his way home.

Caught the train back to Cannes and spent a few more days there before heading back to my field.

Afterward

On, May 8, 1945 the war in Europe officially ended and I anticipated receiving orders to return to the United States.

Within a few days word came down that all pilots who had completed 100 missions would immediately be returned stateside and the rest of us would be rotated over the next few months. While we waited for our orders we were given the assignment of gathering aircraft from fields in Germany and France and flying them to designated disposal points in France.

Some of the aircraft that we were obligated to fly were in such bad condition that this duty was almost as dangerous as flying missions.

Finally in September of 1945 I received my orders to return to the United States. I was fortunate enough to be sent to Southampton, England where I boarded the Queen Mary for what turned out to be a record voyage. There were 15,000 American troops on board and in only 4 ½ days we arrived in New York harbor. We took turns sharing bunks to sleep and waited in Mess Hall lines for food, but nobody cared..........WE WERE GOING HOME.

Late September I received my Honorable Discharge from the Army Air Corps at Fort Dix, New Jersey

After the war Judy and I moved to Levittown, Long Island and I worked for Bill Levitt, the developer. Years later I owned a weekly newspaper called Levittown Press and finally started a direct mail advertising company that proudly had Publishers Clearing House,

Salvation Army and many New York advertising agencies as clients.

I was President of the Mail Advertising Service Association in New York and a member of the Salvation Army Advisory Board.

Made in the USA
San Bernardino, CA
13 January 2020